Cooking with Coconut Flour

A Delicious Low-Carb, Gluten-Free Alternative to Wheat

Bruce Fife, N.D.

Piccadilly Books, Ltd.
Colorado Springs, CO

Every effort has been made to ensure that the information contained in this book is complete and accurate. However, neither the publisher nor the author is engaged in rendering professional advice or services to the individual reader. The ideas, procedures, and suggestions contained in this book are not intended as a substitute for consulting with your physician. All matters regarding your health require medical supervision. Neither the author nor the publisher shall be liable or responsible for any loss of damage allegedly arising from any information or suggestion in this book.

The recipes contained in this book are to be followed exactly as written. The publisher is not responsible for your specific health or allergy needs that may require medical supervision. The publisher is not responsible for any adverse reactions to the recipes contained in this book.

Piccadilly Books, Ltd.
P.O. Box 25203
Colorado Springs, CO 80936, USA
info@piccadillybooks.com
www.piccadillybooks.com

Library of Congress Cataloging-in-Publication Data

Fife, Bruce, 1952-
  Cooking with coconut flour : a delicious low-carb, gluten-free alternative to wheat / by Bruce Fife.
      p. cm.
  Includes bibliographical references and index.
  ISBN-13: 978-0-941599-63-4
  ISBN-10: 0-941599-63-9
  1. Cookery (Coconut flour) 2. Gluten-free diet—Recipes. 3. Wheat-free diet—Recipes. I. Title.
  TX814.5.C63F54 2005
  641.5'63—dc22

                                        2005009388

Printed in the USA

ରେ୨ବ

Contents

1

Coconut Flour

I love wheat and all the things that are made from it: cakes, cookies, pies, pasta, pancakes, muffins; the list goes on and on. Wheat products are one of the most popular foods in our diet. Wheat, in one form or another, is eaten in just about every meal.

If wheat was suddenly removed from our diet, most of us would be at a complete loss. We wouldn't know how to prepare meals without it. The thought of completely eliminating wheat is daunting. Yet, many people are faced with this challenge. Some people are allergic to wheat or cannot tolerate gluten—the protein in many grains. Others avoid wheat and grains to cut down on their carbohydrate intake to improve their health or lose excess weight. For whatever reason you may want to avoid wheat, planning meals without it is a challenging task.

In an attempt to solve this problem, food manufacturers have developed a variety of wheat-free or low-carb breads and flours. These wheat alternatives are made from legumes, potatoes, nuts, and seeds. The problem with most of these products is that if they are gluten-free, they are usually high in carbohydrates, if they are low in carbohydrates, they contain added gluten. Few wheat alternatives are both gluten-free and low in carbohydrates. Soy flour comes the closest. It is high in protein and fiber, but unless it is highly refined and combined with flavor enhancers and additives, soy has a less than desirable taste and texture. In addition, current medical research is showing that consumption of excess soy protein can lead to many health problems including hypothyroidism, dementia, and hormonal imbalances. It's ironic that many people who are on low-carb diets to lose weight are eating soy, which promotes hypothyroidism and weight gain! For these reasons, many people are now trying to avoid soy. Most low-carb, gluten-free alternatives to wheat are very expensive and, honestly, don't taste that good, unless they are loaded with flavor enhancers and sweeteners of one type or another.

Coconut flour provides a suitable solution. Coconut is naturally low in digestible carbohydrate, contains no gluten, is cheaper than most other nut flours, is loaded with health promoting fiber and important nutrients, and tastes terrific. Coconut flour is made from finely ground coconut meat with most of the moisture and fat removed. This flour can be used much like wheat flour to make a multitude of delicious breads, pies, cookies, cakes, snacks, and desserts as well as main dishes. Coconut flour contains less carbohydrate than soy or other nut flours. It contains more calorie-free fiber than other wheat alternatives. Coconut flour also provides a good source of protein. While coconut flour does not contain gluten—the type of protein found in many grains—it does not lack protein. It contains more protein than enriched white flour, rye flour, or cornmeal and about as much as buckwheat and whole wheat flours.

Breads made with coconut flour are light and soft and have a wonderful taste and texture. In this book you will find recipes that will show you how to make a variety of breads and other foods that taste every bit as good, if not better, than those made with wheat.

Before trying any of the recipes in this book, however, I highly recommend that you read the "How to Use Coconut Flour" section toward the end of this chapter. In this section you will learn important characteristics of coconut flour and how to use it successfully in food preparation.

FOOD ALLERGIES

Coconut is ideal for individuals with food allergies. Coconut is regarded as hypoallergenic because few people are allergic to it. It is recommended for those who are allergic to nuts, wheat, soy, milk, and other common allergens. People with allergies to these foods can generally use coconut freely and without fear.

People who are allergic to wheat or dairy are often given substitutes made from soy flour or soy milk. Soybean oil and margarine are recommended in place of butter—a dairy product. But many people are also allergic to soy. What are they to do? Coconut flour, coconut milk, and coconut oil come to the rescue. Coconut provides flour, milk, and oil that can replace wheat, dairy, and soy.

Alternatives to common allergens are often unhealthy. It does little good to remove allergens only to replace them with foods that may eventually do you harm. Although unhealthy foods may not cause allergic reactions, they damage your health just the same. In fact, they are more sinister because they don't cause immediate reactions like allergens do. Their effects appear gradually. When you suffer a heart attack or stroke or develop diabetes, the process is gradual, and our foods are often never suspected.

Many people now avoid soy and particularly soy milk, soy protein, and tofu because of the growing concern about its detrimental affects on health.

Margarine and shortening are often recommended in place of butter or animal fats. But margarine and shortening are hydrogenated oils and contain toxic trans fatty acids—man-made fats that promote heart disease, diabetes, obesity, and numerous other health problems. Real butter is far better for you. If, however, you are allergic to dairy, then coconut oil is your best choice.

Aspartame (Nutrisweet), Splenda, or other non-caloric artificial sweeteners are often recommended to replace sugar in order to cut down on calories. But these chemical sweeteners are foreign to our bodies and they too can lead to health problems.

Many people are in a dilemma. They want to avoid certain foods but the alternatives aren't much better. This book has the answer. Coconut flour provides an alternative to wheat that is high in health promoting fiber and low in digestible carbohydrate. The recipes are good for those who have various types of food allergies, yet still want meals that are healthy and satisfying.

All recipes in this book are:
Wheat-free
Gluten-free
Soy-free
Trans fat-free
Artificial sweetener-free
Yeast-free

Most of the recipes are or can be:
Low sugar
Low carb

Most of the recipes give you the option of using coconut oil or butter, sugar or stevia (a natural non-caloric sweetener) or another sweetener. Most, but not all, recipes are dairy free, relying on coconut milk in place of cow's milk or cream. Wholesome, natural ingredients are recommended over artificial or highly processed ones. The results are foods that are healthy and delicious.

EATING GLUTEN-FREE

Gluten is a protein found in wheat, rye, barley, and oats. These grains are well suited for bread making because of the gluten. Grains with the highest gluten content produce the most desirable breads. Gluten is important because it has an elastic character, which allows dough to hold together and trap air bubbles, making bread soft and light. Without gluten breads tend be heavy and dense.

Although gluten makes wonderful bread, not all people can stomach it. Some people just cannot tolerate gluten. It throws their digestive systems out of kilter. The name for this condition is celiac disease, also known as celiac sprue or gluten-sensitive enteropathy. Celiac disease is a condition in which the lining of the small intestine is damaged by gluten. The damage causes malabsorption of many important nutrients, resulting in weight loss and vitamin and mineral deficiencies, which can lead to a variety of health problems.

Exactly how gluten damages the intestinal lining is not fully understood. However, it seems to be due to an abnormal immunological response. The immune system becomes sensitized to gluten and reacts in the same way it would to an infection or antigen. The abnormal reaction is limited to the intestinal lining. The ability of the cells, which line the intestinal wall, to absorb nutrients is seriously impaired.

The proportion of people affected by the disease varies widely among different countries and populations. In the United States it is estimated that 1 out of every 133 people are affected. Celiac disease tends to run in families, relatives are much more likely than other people to have the disease themselves, which suggests that genetic factors may be involved.

The severity of the disease varies, and many people never develop noticeable symptoms. These people can go through life without realizing they are not absorbing nutrients properly and unknowingly experience subclinical levels of malnutrition. The root cause of many of the health problems they experience in life may go unrecognized. Consequently, they never overcome conditions that eventually become chronic and progressively worse over time.

In adults, symptoms usually develop gradually over months or even years. They range from vague tiredness and breathlessness (due to anemia) to weight loss, diarrhea, gas, vomiting, abdominal pain, and swelling of the legs. Vitamin and mineral deficiencies can lead to a whole host of health problems seemingly unrelated to diet or digestion. In some patients, the damage to the intestinal lining is minimal, but a chronic, distinctive blistering rash called dermatitis herpetiformis develops.

The only effective known treatment is complete lifelong abstinence from gluten. All foods containing wheat (including durum, semolina, kamut, spelt), rye, and barley must be avoided. Although oats contain gluten, this type of gluten doesn't appear to cause harm and most celiacs can safely eat oats. There is no restriction on meat, fish, eggs, dairy, vegetables, fruit, rice, or corn.

When gluten is removed from the diet, the lining of the intestine has a chance to heal. Within a few weeks symptoms generally clear up and the sufferer starts to regain lost weight and to enjoy normal health. Although health improves, gluten cannot be reintroduced into the diet. Gluten sensitivity is a permanent condition and it must be avoided for life.

Removing gluten from the diet is not easy. Grains are used in the preparation of many of the foods we love and eat every day. Bread is a staple for most people. Wheat flour and other grains are used to make numerous foods ranging from cakes and pies to frozen dinners and processed meats. You must read ingredient labels carefully.

Most of us tend to eat wheat in one form or another every day. Eliminating it completely from the diet is no small task. Many of those on gluten-free diets miss the breads and baked goods they learned to enjoy as children. Fortunately, food manufacturers have created a variety of gluten-free breads and other foods that are similar to those they once enjoyed.

A large proportion of commercially prepared gluten-free foods are made using soy flour. Soy flour is rich in protein and is a good source of dietary fiber. In recent years, however, soy protein has fallen out of favor. People are now looking for gluten-free alternatives to soy. Nut flours, such as almond flour, have become more popular but they are expensive and few people can afford to eat them regularly. There are a variety of other flours such as potato flour, garbanzo flour, rice flour, etc. Gluten-free bread recipes often require the combination of three, four, or even five different types of flour along with an assortment of conditioners, stabilizers, and gums to make a loaf of bread that is an acceptable substitute to wheat bread.

Gluten-free bread making doesn't have to be a costly or a complicated process involving a dozen different ingredients. An ideal gluten-free alternative to wheat is coconut flour. You can make a variety of excellent tasting breads using little more than coconut flour, eggs, and oil. The recipes are simple and easy to follow

HIGH-FIBER, LOW-CARB

Two types of carbohydrate occur in foods: digestible and non-digestible. Digestible carbohydrate consists of starch and sugar and provides calories. Non-digestible carbohydrate is simply dietary fiber. Fiber, for the most part, is not broken down or digested in humans and provides no calories.

The type of carbohydrates that are of concern to most people are digestible carbohydrates—the starch and sugar in our foods. These are the carbs that the body converts into fat and packs into our fat cells. These are the carbs that, when eaten in excess, contribute to an assortment of health problems such as insulin resistance, obesity, and diabetes. These are the carbs that people on low-carb diets try to avoid.

Non-digestible carbohydrate, on the other hand, passes through the digestive tract without being broken down or absorbed and is passed out of the body essentially unaltered. Instead of contributing to health problems like starch and sugar do, fiber promotes good health. Most of

11

us don't eat enough fiber, and nutritionists encourage us to increase our fiber intake. The best way to do this is by eating foods rich in fiber such as whole grains, vegetables, and fruits.

Whole grains such as wheat and rye are some of the richest sources of fiber. Grains contain more fiber than fruits and vegetables. However, for people who cannot tolerate gluten, these grains aren't an option.

Coconut is a natural low-carb, high-fiber food ideally suited for low-carbohydrate diets. One cup of shredded fresh coconut (80 grams) contains a mere 3 grams of digestible carbohydrate and 9 grams of fiber. The remaining 68 grams consists primarily of water, fat, and protein. Although a piece of fresh coconut may taste sweet, its digestible carbohydrate content is lower, and its fiber content higher than most fruits and vegetables. Coconut has three times as much fiber as it does digestible carbohydrate. In comparison, a similar volume of green beans contains 7 grams of digestible carbohydrate and only 3 grams of fiber. A carrot has 8 grams of digestible carbohydrate and only 4 grams of fiber. Table 1 on the following page compares the carbohydrate and fiber content of various foods.

Plant foods contain a mixture of both digestible and non-digestible carbohydrate. The right hand column in Table 1 lists the percentage of total carbohydrate in each food that consists of fiber. Coconut has one of the highest percentages of fiber among all plant foods. Seventy-five percent of the total carbohydrate content is fiber. In comparison, the carbohydrate in green beans is only 30 percent fiber, corn is only 18 percent fiber, and bananas a mere 9 percent.

Some foods contain more *total* fiber than coconut, but they also have a high amount of digestible carbohydrate. Although rich in fiber, such foods are restricted in most low-carb diets. Legumes are a great source of fiber, but they are loaded with digestible carbohydrate. A cup of black beans, for example, has 15 grams of fiber with 26 grams of digestible carbohydrate. The fiber content is only 37 percent. Compare this to the 75 percent in coconut. For those people trying to restrict carbohydrate intake, coconut is by far a better source of fiber because it doesn't have the added starch and sugar.

Like whole coconut, coconut flour is rich in fiber but low in digestible carbohydrate. Coconut flour is made from finely ground, dried, and defatted coconut. Coconut flour has far more fiber than any other flour.

12

Table 1. Carbohydrate Content of Various Foods

Food	Digestible Carbs(g/cup)	Fiber (g/cup)	Percent Fiber
Coconut	3	9	75
Turnip	2	4	67
Broccoli	4	6	60
Kale	3	4	57
Spinach	3	4	57
Asparagus	4	4	50
Bean sprouts	3	3	50
Cabbage	2	2	50
Cauliflower	2	2	50
Celery	2	2	50
Kidney beans	20	19	49
Peanuts	14	13	48
Macadamia	10	7	41
Filbert (hazelnut)	11	7	39
Tomato	5	3	38
Peas	21	12	36
Strawberries	7	4	36
Pecans	13	7	35
Beets	8	4	33
Bell pepper	4	2	33
Carrot	8	4	33
Kelp	16	8	33
Walnuts	15	7	32
Lima beans	22	10	31
Green beans	7	3	30
Sunflower seeds	20	8	29
Okra	12	4	25
Garbanzo	34	11	24
Onion	11	3	21
Blueberries	17	4	19
Cashew	37	8	18
Corn	28	6	18
Papaya	12	2	14
Pineapple	17	2	11
Banana	32	3	9
Watermelon	11	1	8

Wheat bran is often recommended as a supplemental source of dietary fiber. It is an excellent source of fiber. However, coconut flour has over twice as much fiber as wheat bran. It has 4 times as much as oat bran or soy flour, and 20 times as much as enriched white bread (see graph below).

Besides having significantly more fiber than other flours, coconut flour tastes a whole lot better than wheat bran, soy flour, or any other high fiber flour. When used in baking, it can be just as light and taste just as good as wheat flour.

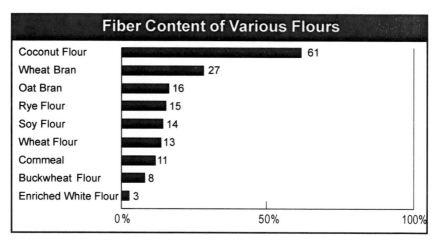

Coconut flour contains the highest percentage of dietary fiber in comparison to other flours. Sixty-one percent of the flour consists of fiber with water, protein, fat, and carbohydrate making up the remaining 39 percent.

BENEFITS OF COCONUT FIBER
Why Fiber is Good For You
The importance of fiber in the diet was first noted by physicians working in Africa, India, and Oceania in the early and mid-twentieth century. They observed that people eating traditional diets, high in fiber, enjoyed a level of health better than those in Western countries. Absent were

the health problems commonly seen in Europe and America. However, when these people began eating Western foods, rich in low fiber refined grains and sugar, their health deteriorated and they developed many of same health problems commonly found in the West.

Physicians noticed that in rural communities where fiber intake was high, degenerative disease was low. Where fiber consumption was low, due to the use of modern foods, disease rates were much higher. This observation led to what is known as the "fiber hypothesis" which suggests that the consumption of unrefined, high-fiber foods protect against many degenerative health problems common in Western countries.

British surgeon and epidemiologist Denis Burkitt, MD was the leading proponent of the fiber hypothesis. Working in rural Africa beginning in the 1940s Burkitt observed that the bowel habits of rural Africans were very different from those of the British. Africans passed soft, odorless stools four times the weight of the British. He noted that in Africans, food traveled through their digestive tracts and was expelled in as little as one day, compared to a full three or more days for the British. The Africans' diet consisted primarily of high-fiber foods such as cereals, beans, peas, and root vegetables. In contrast, the British diet was composed predominately of refined grains and sugar. The researchers calculated that Africans consumed four to five times as much fiber as the British. This high-fiber diet accounted for the African's large, soft, frequent bowel movements. The significance of their bowel habits was recognized when it was observed that many of the digestive problems common in Britain were completely absent among the African villagers. Not only were there fewer digestive problems, but they were also free from most all other non-infectious diseases as well, such as heart disease, diabetes, and obesity. Dietary fiber, it was reasoned, must have some connection to overall health beyond just bowel function.

It became apparent that the most striking consequence of not having enough fiber in the diet was constipation. Based on his studies in Africa and elsewhere Burkitt drew a direct connection between constipation and five other common health problems: diverticular disease, appendicitis, hiatal hernia, hemorrhoids, and varicose veins. Each of these, he said, was caused by straining to expel hard fecal matter.

Fiber is important because it regulates bowel activity. It absorbs water, providing a medium that is moist and mobile which can speedily sweep the inside of the bowel clean. Fiber, in essence, is nature's way of keeping our intestines clean, healthy, and functioning smoothly.

A diet low in fiber and, consequently, high in refined, overly processed foods leads to constipation, which in turn, can set the stage for a number of health problems. Excessive pressures caused by hardened fecal material can damage tissues within the colon. Pressures can become so great trying to move this hardened mass through the colon that tissues in the intestinal wall break down, give way, and begin to bulge, sometimes forming pockets that fill with hardened waste. These pockets of fecal waste are called diverticula. People can have literally dozens of diverticula ranging in size from a fingertip to a tennis ball. A person who has many of them is said to have diverticular disease or diverticulosis. After the age of 40 one half of all Americans develop diverticular disease. In his 20 years working in Africa Dr. Burkitt says he did not see a single case of diverticular disease.

High pressure caused by the sluggish movement of waste can weaken and deform the colon, causing bulging, stretching, and tears in the lining of the bowel. These conditions can lead not only to diverticulosis but also to appendicitis, hemorrhoids, hiatal hernia, varicose veins, prolapsed colon, heartburn, even gallstones, and may contribute to ulcerative colitis and Crohn's disease.

Since the fiber hypothesis was first proposed, a host of other conditions characteristic of modern Western civilization have been shown to be related to intestinal transit time (the time it takes food to pass through the digestive tract). Adding more fiber into the diet, preferably by eating more high fiber foods and fewer low fiber ones, has proven to be beneficial. Coconut is an excellent source of health-promoting dietary fiber. Research suggests that coconut and particularly coconut dietary fiber may help prevent and treat:

Constipation and diarrhea
Hemorrhoids
Appendicitis
Diverticulosis

Varicose veins
Hiatal hernia
Gallstones
Irritable bowel syndrome
Colitis and Crohn's disease
Heartburn
Obesity
Candidiasis
Intestinal parasites
Heart disease and stroke
High cholesterol
High blood pressure
Hypoglycemia (low blood sugar)
Diabetes
Colon cancer
Breast cancer
Prostate cancer
Ovarian cancer

Weight Management
Since you cannot digest dietary fiber, you do not derive any calories from it. Dietary fiber is calorie-free. You can eat as much as you like without worrying about gaining weight—good news for those who are concerned about their weight.

Fiber absorbs water like a sponge. For this reason it aids in filling the stomach and producing a feeling of fullness. It provides bulk without supplying fat-promoting calories. Fiber also slows down the emptying of the stomach, thus maintaining the feeling of fullness longer than low-fiber foods. As a result, less food and fewer calories are consumed.

Studies have shown that consumption of an additional 14 grams of fiber a day (the amount in about ¼ cup of coconut flour) is associated with a 10 percent decrease in calorie intake and a loss in body weight. The observed changes occur both when the fiber is from high-fiber foods, like fresh vegetables or coconut, or when it is from products made with high-fiber flours, such as coconut flour.

When you eat high-fiber foods that are generally low in calories, you crowd out higher calorie foods. Simply adding high-fiber foods to your diet will lower your calorie intake even if you eat the same volume of food you normally do. This fact was demonstrated by a study in which a group of overweight men were asked to eat 12 slices of whole wheat bread each day in addition to whatever other foods they wanted to eat. They could eat any other food they desired—desserts, meats, cream—it didn't matter as long as it was food they normally ate. The study lasted for three months. At the end of the study the volunteers lost an average of 19.4 pounds. As long as they consumed the required amount of whole wheat bread, they were allowed to eat as much as they wanted. The bread was so filling that they didn't want a lot of other foods. Eating baked goods made with coconut flour provides more fiber than whole wheat, without the gluten and without the carbohydrate! If the researchers used coconut flour products in place of whole wheat bread, the volunteers' total weight loss would probably have been even greater.

Studies have shown that populations that rely heavily on coconut do not have weight problems. For example, in a study reported in *The American Journal of Clinical Nutrition* a Pacific island population of 203 individuals ages 20 to 86 were examined. Researchers noted that they were all lean despite an abundance of food. These people ate as much as they wanted, but overweight problems did not exist because their diet was rich in fiber, particularly from coconut.

Since fiber absorbs fluids, it is recommend that you drink plenty of water when you eat foods made with coconut flour. The fiber in the flour will absorb the liquid causing it to swell and increase in size and bulk. Your stomach will feel full sooner so you will be inclined to eat less and, therefore, consume fewer calories. This feeling of satisfaction will remain longer than with other foods, lessening the desire to snack between meals. If you do not drink enough liquids with the fiber, you may become constipated. So drink plenty of fluids. Fiber and water don't have any calories. They can fill you up and keep you from consuming too many foods that do have calories. Adding both coconut fiber and water to your diet can be an excellent means to help you lose excess pounds without feeling starved. With all the delicious recipes in this book, you won't feel deprived either.

Intestinal Environment

Our intestines are teaming with bacteria. Most of these bacteria are beneficial to us. These bacteria produce vitamins and other substances that nourish the cells in the intestinal wall, improve nutrient absorption, and promote good health. In fact, an abundance of these microflora are essential to our health. The intestinal tract is also home to some unfriendly microflora—bacteria and yeasts that can cause harm. In a healthy digestive tract the friendly bacteria far outnumber the harmful ones and keep these troublemakers under control.

Good bacteria flourish when we eat high-fiber foods. Fiber is their primary source of nourishment. When your diet contains an adequate amount of fiber, the good bacteria are happy and they dominate your digestive tract. If you do not eat enough fiber, the good bacteria decrease in number. Harmful bacteria and yeasts, which thrive on sugar and refined carbohydrates, flourish. The environment inside the intestines becomes unbalanced. These harmful microflora damage the intestinal wall and produce toxic byproducts that can be absorbed into the bloodstream and sent throughout the body. This can lead to food allergies, nutrient deficiencies, abnormal growths, candidiasis, and an assortment of health problems that appear to be unrelated to digestive function such as arthritis, dermatitis, and depression.

Inflammatory bowel disease (IBD), which includes irritable bowel syndrome, Crohn's disease, and ulcerative colitis, occurs when the intestinal environment is out of balance. These conditions are characterized by abdominal pain, nausea, indigestion, excessive gas, and chronic dirrahea. Consuming even a small amount of coconut can be helpful. Many people with IBD have reported that eating as little as two coconut macaroon cookies a day relieves their symptoms. Eating two coconut cookies a day—what a pleasant and easy way to stop the pain and discomfort caused by inflammatory bowel disease.

Eating an adequate amount of fiber daily helps to keep friendly organisms healthy and unfriendly ones at bay. An interesting benefit of coconut fiber, not found in other fibers, is that it can expel intestinal worms. Eating coconut meat to get rid of parasites is a traditional practice in India that was recognized among the early medical profession and is still used in some parts of the country today. Researchers have tested this method and have found that eating a sufficient quantity of coconut can expel over 90 percent of intestinal parasites within 12 hours. Dried coconut is more effective than fresh in removing tapeworms. The researchers recommend eating foods made with coconut flour, a form of dried coconut, as a safe and relatively easy way to treat tapeworm infestation.

Heart Health

If you want to protect yourself from heart disease, you should include ample amounts of fiber in your diet. A multitude of studies have demonstrated that dietary fiber protects against heart attacks and strokes.

Part of the reason why dietary fiber protects the heart is that it reduces many of the risk factors associated with heart disease. Some forms of fiber, such as that found in oat bran and coconut flour, help reduce cholesterol, thus reducing risk of heart disease. Blood pressure is also influenced by dietary fiber. Even a modest increase in fiber intake results in a significant decrease in blood pressure. Another risk factor affected by fiber is diabetes. People with diabetes are much more prone to heart disease than the general population. Dietary fiber is known to increase insulin sensitivity, thus reducing symptoms associated with diabetes and, consequently, the risk of heart disease.

If you want to avoid a heart attack or a stroke, you should eat more coconut. Coconut flour is heart healthy. It has a positive impact on blood lipid levels and will *lower* your cholesterol. A recent study in *Journal of Medicinal Food* has shown that adding coconut flour into the diet will significantly lower total cholesterol, LDL (bad) cholesterol, and triglycerides. On the other hand, coconut has been shown to increase HDL (good) cholesterol. So the total lipid profile improves, reducing risk of heart disease. These effects have been observed in both animal and human studies.

Coconut meat not only protects the heart by modifying blood lipid levels, but it also improves antioxidant status and reduces oxidative stress. Antioxidants protect tissues such as the heart and blood vessels from the destructive action of free radicals. Studies have shown that coconut consumption decreases oxidation products in the heart and increases the activity of superoxide dismutase and catalase—antioxidant

20

enzymes that protect the heart and arteries from free radicals that promote atherosclerosis.

Blood Sugar and Diabetes

Blood sugar is an important issue for anyone who is concerned about heart disease, overweight, hypoglycemia, and especially diabetes because it affects all of these conditions.

Carbohydrates in our foods are broken down in the digestive tract and converted into glucose (blood sugar). A certain amount of glucose in the blood is necessary for normal function. However, if blood glucose concentration falls too low or rises too high, it can cause many health problems and in severe cases it will lead to a coma and death. For this reason, the body strives to maintain blood sugar levels within a narrow range of values. If blood glucose rises above this range, more insulin is produced. Insulin is a hormone that transfers glucose from the blood and into the cells where it is burned to produce energy. If blood sugar drops below normal, the body produces another hormone called glucagon. Glucagon opposes the action of insulin by stimulating the release of sugar into the blood stream. In this manner swings in blood sugar are quickly rebalanced and maintained at normal levels.

Meals that contain a high concentration of carbohydrates, particularly simple carbohydrates such as sugar and refined flours, cause a rapid rise in blood sugar. Since elevated blood sugar can lead to a coma, insulin is frantically pumped into the blood stream to avoid this condition. If insulin is produced in adequate amounts, blood sugar is soon brought back down to normal. This is what happens in most individuals. However, if insulin is not produced quickly enough or if the cells become desensitized to the action of insulin, blood glucose can remain elevated for extended periods of time, leading to diabetes.

When cells become desensitized to insulin, this is called "insulin resistance" Insulin resistance is a major factor that leads to both diabetes and obesity. One of the causes of insulin resistance is chronic elevated blood sugar that results from eating too much carbohydrate. If a person is always eating sweets, white bread, and other high carbohydrate foods, blood sugar and insulin are continually elevated. This constant exposure to insulin desensitizes the cells so that they become less responsive to the hormone's action. Therefore, more insulin is required to lower blood sugar to normal levels. Symptoms associated with diabetes are a consequence of blood sugar that is out of balance.

Dietary fiber helps moderate swings in blood sugar by slowing down the absorption of sugar into the blood stream. This helps keep blood sugar and insulin levels under control. Drs. Anderson and Gustafson of the University of Kentucky and the Endocrine-Metabolic Section of the Veterans Administration Medical Center in Lexington report that a high-fiber diet helps reduce the need for insulin to the extent that fiber eliminates the need for insulin injections for two-thirds of patients who develop diabetes in later years. They report that a high-fiber diet cuts back by 25 percent the amount of insulin needed by diabetics whose diabetes began in childhood.

Coconut fiber has been shown to be very effective in moderating blood sugar and insulin levels. For this reason, coconut is good for diabetics. Diabetics are encouraged to eat foods that have a relatively low glycemic index. The glycemic index is a measure of how foods affect blood sugar levels. The higher the glycemic index, the greater an effect a particular food has on raising blood sugar. So diabetics need to eat foods with a low glycemic index. When coconut is added to foods, including those high in starch and sugar, it *lowers* the glycemic index of these foods. This was clearly demonstrated by T. P. Trinidad and colleagues in a study published in the *British Journal of Nutrition*. In their study, both normal and diabetic subjects were given a variety of foods to eat. Some of the types of food included cinnamon bread, granola bars, carrot cake, and brownies—all foods that a diabetic must ordinarily limit because of their high sugar and starch content. The researchers found that as the coconut content of the foods increased, the blood sugar response between the diabetic and non-diabetic subjects became nearly identical. In other words, coconut moderated the release of sugar into the bloodstream so that there was no spike in blood glucose levels. As the coconut content in the foods decreased, the diabetic subjects' blood sugar levels became elevated, as would normally be expected from eating foods high in sugar and white flour. This study showed that adding coconut to foods lowers the glycemic index of the foods and keeps blood sugar levels under control.

It is interesting, that before Western foods were routinely shipped to the islands of the Pacific, diabetes was unheard of among the islanders. These people lived on coconut-based diets, eating mostly sweet fruits and starchy vegetables. Although they ate a high-carbohydrate diet, they did not have blood sugar problems. Only after they began to take on Western eating habits, low in fiber, did diabetes begin to appear.

Even though many of the recipes in this book contain sugar or fruit, because of the glycemic lowering effect of the coconut flour, blood sugar levels remain relatively steady. You can feel comfortable eating the foods in this book, especially the reduced sugar versions, without worrying about your blood sugar going out of control.

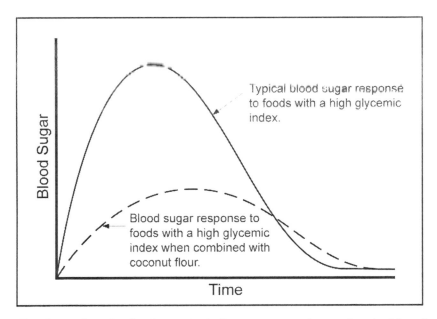

Foods with a high glycemic index cause a sharp rise in blood sugar level. These same foods combined with coconut flour produce a moderate blood sugar response.

Cancer Prevention

Fiber acts like a broom, sweeping the intestinal contents through the digestive tract. Parasites, toxins, and carcinogens are swept along with the fiber, leading to their timely expulsion from the body. This cleansing action helps prevent toxins that irritate intestinal tissues and cause cancer from getting lodged in the intestinal tract. Colon cancer is second only to lung cancer as the world's most deadly form of cancer. Many studies have shown a correlation between high-fiber diets and a low incidence of colon cancer. For example, one of the most extensive studies to date, involving over 400,000 people from nine European countries, demonstrated that those who had the highest fiber intake were 40 percent less likely to develop colon cancer.

Fiber readily absorbs fluids. It also appears to absorb harmful carcinogens and other toxic substances. Researchers at the University of Lund, Sweden, found that fiber in the diet can absorb toxins that promote cancer. Various types of fiber were examined for their absorption capacity and found to soak up to 20 to 50 percent of these carcinogenic compounds.

Dr. B. H. Ershoff of Loma Linda University summarized studies reported by the Committee on Nutrition in Medical Education. The studies compared groups of rats and mice, some given high-fiber diets and others given low-fiber diets. The animals were fed various drugs, chemicals, and food additives. These substances proved to be poisonous to the animals on the low-fiber diets, yet those given high-fiber diets showed no deleterious effects.

Logically you can see the relationship between dietary fiber and its protective effect in the colon, but studies also show it protects against breast, prostate, and ovarian cancers as well. One explanation for this is that toxins lingering in the colon are absorbed into the bloodstream, and the blood then carries these toxins to other parts of the body where they can cause cancer.

Another explanation involves estrogen. Estrogen is required for the early growth and development of breast and ovarian cancers. The liver collects estrogen and sends it into the intestines where it is reabsorbed into the bloodstream. A high-fiber diet interrupts this process. Less estrogen is allowed back into the bloodstream because the activities

24

of bacterial enzymes in the intestine are reduced. Studies show that serum estrogen can be significantly reduced by a high-fiber diet. Progesterone, which is an antagonist to estrogen and helps protect against cancer, is not affected or reduced by fiber.

One of the primary reasons given to explain why dietary fiber protects against colon and other cancers is that it increases intestinal transit time. If carcinogenic substances, hormones, and toxins are quickly moved through the digestive tract and out of the body, they don't get a chance to irritate tissues and instigate cancer. Coconut fiber not only absorbs and sweeps carcinogenic toxins out of the intestinal tract, it also helps prevent the conditions that promote cancer. Evidence suggests that coconut fiber may also prevent the formation of tumors in the colon by moderating the harmful effects of tumor-promoting enzymes.

Mineral Availability and Absorption

Most grains are grown in mineral depleted soils. Farmlands have been used repeatedly for so many years that the mineral content is very poor, especially in trace minerals. Fertilizers supply nitrogen, phosphorus, and potassium that make plants grow big and green, but they do not supply trace minerals. Trace minerals come from the breakdown of rock. As rock disintegrates, these minerals are released into the soil. Plants absorb these minerals. We, in turn, get these minerals by eating the plants. If the soil doesn't contain these minerals, neither do the plants. Many areas of the world lack important trace minerals like iodine and selenium. For this reason, people can experience trace mineral deficiencies. A deficiency in iodine can lead to goiter and a deficiency in selenium can lead to heart disease and increase the risk of cancer. Soils have become so depleted in iodine that at one time goiter was a serious problem in North America. It still is a problem in many parts of the world. For the most part, we have overcome this problem by adding iodine to table salt. That may solve the iodine problem but there are dozens of other trace minerals important to human health that are not available from foods grown on mineral depleted farmlands.

Coconut is a good source of many trace minerals. Coconuts generally grow in mineral rich volcanic soils. These soils are also enriched by minerals from seawater. In fact, seawater is an important natural fertilizer for coconut palms. Seawater contains a complete mixture of all the trace minerals needed by the human body. Coconut flour can provide trace minerals that may be lacking in other flours derived from grains grown on overworked and depleted soils.

Some plants, even if they are grown in mineral rich soils, may not supply an adequate amount of trace minerals. The fiber in our foods can influence mineral absorption. The foods with the highest fiber content are legumes and grains like soy, wheat, and oats. One drawback that has been reported by researchers with the bran or fiber from these sources is that they contain phytic acid, which binds with minerals in the digestive tract and pulls them out of the body. Consequently, mineral absorption is decreased. Some of the minerals that are bound to phytic acid include zinc, iron, and calcium. It has been suggested that eating too much food containing phytic acid can lead to mineral deficiencies. Even dietary fiber levels of 10 to 20 percent interfere with absorption of minerals in the digestive tract. Yet, we are counseled to get between 20 and 35 percent dietary fiber in our diets. What are we to do? We need fiber for good digestive health, but too much may cause nutritional problems. The perfect solution to this problem is not to reduce fiber consumption, but to replace some of the fiber we get from grains and legumes with fiber that does not pull minerals out of the body. Coconut fiber fits that description. Coconut does not contain phytic acid and does not remove minerals from the body. You can eat all the coconut you want without worrying about it negatively affecting your mineral status.

If anything, coconut flour improves mineral status. Fiber slows down the emptying of the stomach, allowing foods to be bathed in gastric juices for a longer amount of time. This allows more minerals to be released from the food we eat. So more minerals are available for absorption. Also, coconut flour contains a small amount of oil. Coconut oil is known to improve the absorption of many important minerals, including calcium and magnesium.

BENEFITS OF COCONUT OIL
Many of the recipes in this book use a fair amount of fat. Coconut flour contains about 10 percent oil, which is a little higher than most other

flours. Coconut oil or butter are also used in many of the recipes in this book. Some people worry that if they add fat to their diets, they will be consuming extra calories and end up gaining weight. This is not so. In fact, just the opposite happens. This is particularly true with coconut oil.

When I tell people that using coconut oil can help them lose weight, they look at me in shock. They question: how can fat help me lose fat? Isn't fat supposed to make you gain weight? Fat isn't the culprit. Sugar and refined carbohydrates are a much bigger problem. You will be more successful losing unwanted weight by reducing the amount of carbohydrates you eat than you would by reducing the fat. In fact, adding an adequate amount of fat into your diet can help you lose weight. The best fat to use for weight loss is coconut oil. Because of its effect on weight management, coconut oil has gained a reputation as being the world's only natural, low-calorie fat.

Coconut oil is unique. It is composed of a special group of fat molecules known as medium-chain triglycerides (MCTs). MCTs are digested and metabolized differently from other fats. Instead of being packed away into fat cells, MCTs are used to produce energy This boost in energy production stimulates metabolism. As metabolism increases, the rate at which you burn calories increases. So after eating a meal containing coconut oil, your level of energy is higher, your metabolism is running at an elevated level, and you burn calories at an accelerated rate. Since more calories are burned up to produce energy, fewer calories remain to be converted into body fat. Adding coconut oil to your foods actually reduces the effective amount of calories in the food. In other words, since coconut oil causes the body to burn more calories, adding coconut oil into your foods will reduce the number of calories in the food that are eventually converted into body fat. As long as you don't overeat, coconut oil can help you lose excess pounds.

In addition, coconut oil is very satisfying. When you add it to foods, it satisfies hunger quicker so it helps prevent overeating. It also keeps you from getting hungry afterwards so you are not as inclined to snack between meals. By the end of the day, you tend to consume less food and less calories. Again, you have fewer excess calories that can be converted into body fat.

Coconut oil also helps regulate blood sugar and prevent insulin resistance. Insulin resistance is one of the main causes of weight gain. When you eat carbohydrates, they are broken down into sugar and sent into the bloodstream. This is digestible carbohydrate—sugar and starch—not fiber. The hormone insulin is needed to transfer sugar from the blood and bring it into the cells. The cells use sugar as a source of fuel to power metabolism. Without insulin the sugar would remain in the blood and the cells would starve to death. Your blood could be loaded with sugar, but without insulin none of it would be able to get into the cells where it is needed. Many people become insulin resistant. Their cells become unresponsive to insulin. When this happens, blood sugar rises and cells starve. This leads to a host of health problems including diabetes and obesity.

Have you ever wondered why a thin person can eat a ton of food and not gain an ounce, while you, on the other hand, may eat a cookie and gain five pounds? Or so it seems. The reason is insulin resistance. Most overweight individuals are insulin resistant. For this reason, carbohydrate rich foods are more of a problem, in terms of weight gain, than dietary fat. Fat does not raise blood sugar. Carbohydrates do. When blood sugar rises, signals are sent to increase the production of insulin. If the cells have become resistant to insulin, then a much larger amount of insulin is needed to overcome this resistance and move the sugar into the cells. In insulin resistant individuals, insulin levels rise far above normal and remain elevated for extended amounts of time. One of the problems with this is that insulin also transports fat into fat cells. As insulin levels rise, more fat is packed away into the fat cells. If insulin levels are elevated and remain elevated for extended amounts of time, more fat gets stored in fat cells, and body fat increases. A person with insulin resistance can eat a small amount of carbohydrate and experience weight gain, while an individual who is not insulin resistant may lose weight with the same amount of calories.

Coconut oil is beneficial for both diabetics and those who struggle with weight problems. It helps improve insulin secretion and insulin sensitivity thus reversing the effects of insulin resistance. So not only does coconut oil satisfy hunger and raise metabolism, but it helps improve the utilization of blood sugar and prevent insulin resistance. All of these things working together make coconut oil the best choice of oil for those who are concerned about their weight.

In recent years coconut oil has made a name for itself as one of the "good" fats because it can help protect against many health problems including obesity and diabetes as well as heart disease. At one time, coconut oil had the misfortune of being labeled a dietary troublemaker because it is high in saturated fat. Many people avoided it for that reason. What most people didn't know at the time was that the saturated fat in coconut oil was a unique type of fat composed predominately of medium-chain triglycerides. This fat is completely different from the saturated fat found in meat and other vegetable oils and has a number of health benefits. Ironically, one of the benefits of coconut oil is that it helps protect against heart disease and stroke.

This fact is clearly evident in populations around the world who rely on coconut for food and eat it every day of their lives. For thousands of years people in Southeast Asia, and elsewhere have been consuming coconuts and coconut oil without any ill effect. In these countries heart disease is relatively rare. In fact, those people who eat the most coconut have the lowest heart disease rates in the world. Even though people in the coconut growing regions of the world have consumed coconut oil every day of their lives, heart disease was completely unknown to them until just a few decades ago. Heart disease didn't show up until after they began replacing traditional foods, such as coconut, with Western foods high in sugar and refined grains. Coconut was one of the key ingredients in their diets that protected them from heart disease.

Recent medical research has shown that medium-chain triglycerides possess anti-inflammatory and antioxidant properties, both of which help protect the arteries from clogging up with plaque and the heart from succumbing to heart disease. This research further confirms the observation that those people who eat lots of coconut oil have a low incidence of heart disease.

In traditional forms of medicine around the world, coconut oil is used to treat a wide variety of health problems. One of the most remarkable characteristics of coconut oil is its antimicrobial properties. When eaten, MCTs in coconut oil are transformed by the body into powerful germ-fighting substances that kill disease-causing viruses, bacteria, and fungi. Research has shown that these coconut oil derived substances kill microorganisms that cause sinus infections, pneumonia, bladder infections, candidiasis, influenza, measles, herpes, mononucleosis, hepatitis C, and many other illnesses.

In addition to its germ-fighting capacity, coconut oil strengthens the immune system, improves digestion, protects against cancer, enhances thyroid function, and helps protect against and heal many other health problems. For a more complete discussion on the health benefits of coconut oil I highly recommend my book *The Coconut Oil Miracle*.

HOW TO USE COCONUT FLOUR
Increasing Your Daily Fiber Intake

Nutritionists recommend that we get between 20 to 35 grams of fiber a day. This is 2 to 3 times higher than the average intake for those in most Western countries, which is about 10-14 grams a day. Adding foods containing coconut flour to your diet can significantly improve your daily fiber intake.

You can increase the fiber content of your meals and enjoy many of the health benefits of coconut by simply adding a little coconut flour to the foods you normally eat each day. Research shows that adding even a little fiber to the diet can have a significant influence on health. For example, in a study on cardiovascular disease, a high-fiber diet was associated with a 21 percent lower risk of heart disease. The difference in fiber intake of the subjects wasn't great. The highest intake was only 23 grams, only about 9 or 10 grams above average. You can easily increase the fiber in your diet by 9 or 10 grams by simply adding a few tablespoons of coconut flour to the foods you normally eat each day.

You can do this by adding a tablespoon or two of coconut flour to beverages, smoothies, baked goods, casseroles, soups, and hot cereal. This is a simple and easy way to add fiber into your daily diet without making drastic changes in the way you eat. Another way to add coconut fiber into your diet is by using coconut flour in your baking. There are two ways you can do this. One is to combine a little coconut flour with other flours using standard recipes you find in most cookbooks. The second way is to use the recipes in this book to make baked goods using 100 percent coconut flour. The unique feature about this book is that most of the recipes use only coconut flour.

Using Standard Recipes

Up until recently coconut flour has not been used much for making baked goods. Part of the reason is because it can be difficult to work with if you are unfamiliar with it. Although it looks and feels much like wheat flour, coconut flour does not act the same when used in baking. For this reason, you cannot use 100 percent coconut flour in bread recipes *that are designed* for wheat flour.

Coconut flour lacks gluten, an important ingredient in bread making. Gluten is necessary in baked goods because it makes dough elastic, allowing it to trap and hold air bubbles, which gives wheat bread it characteristic light, airy texture.

Another difference is that coconut flour is much more absorbent than wheat and other flours. One of the characteristics of fiber is its ability to absorb moisture. Because of the very high fiber content of coconut flour, it absorbs significantly more liquid than other flours.

Since coconut flour lacks gluten and is highly absorbent, it cannot be substituted entirely for wheat flour in *standard* recipes. If you tried to make a chocolate cake by replacing all the wheat flour with coconut flour in a standard recipe, you would fail completely. Your cake would be hard and crumbly and taste terrible.

In most cases, coconut flour cannot be substituted completely for wheat or other flours in typical bread recipes. You need to combine it with wheat, rye, or oat flour. When making quick breads, you can generally replace up to 25 percent of the wheat flour with coconut flour, but 10 to 20 percent is better. This still increases the fiber content of your baked goods considerably.

Because coconut flour absorbs more liquid than wheat flour, you will also need to add a little more water to the recipe. As a general rule of thumb, add an equal portion of water or other fluid. If you use ½ cup of coconut flour, add an additional ½ cup of water to the recipe. For example, if the recipe calls for 1 cup of wheat flour and 1 cup of water, you can reduce the wheat flour to ¾ cup and add ¼ cup (25 percent) of coconut flour, but you should then also include ¼ additional cup of water (1¼ cups of water total). This is a general guideline; the best way to judge if you have enough liquid is to look at the batter. If it looks too dry, add a little more liquid.

If you are allergic to wheat or sensitive to gluten, you won't want to use standard bread recipes. In that case, this book will be of great value to you. All of the recipes in this book are wheat free. Coconut flour is the only flour used for most of the recipes in this book.

All-Coconut Flour Baking

I've used wheat flour in baking for many years and have been very successful in making delicious tasting breads, cakes, pies, and assorted goodies. When I began to experiment with using coconut flour, I thought that all I needed to do was to replace the wheat with the coconut flour with only a few minor adjustments. When I used 100 percent coconut flour in my recipes, they were all dismal failures. I only had success if I combined coconut flour with wheat flour. The maximum amount of coconut flour I could use in combination with wheat flour was about 25 percent. Limiting the coconut flour to 15 to 20 percent worked best in most recipes. If more than 25 percent of the wheat was replaced with coconut flour, the character of the product began to change noticeably.

I began looking for recipes that used all coconut flour. I contacted people experienced with using coconut flour and found that the only recipes available were those that used a combination of coconut and wheat flours. They too limited their use to only 20 to 25 percent or less. I couldn't find anyone at the time who knew how to use 100 percent coconut flour successfully to make baked goods.

I continued to experiment. I finally found success when I completely abandoned my wheat recipes and approached the process from a different perspective. Since coconut flour lacks gluten, I needed to add another protein source that could trap and hold air bubbles in a similar manner. Eggs fulfilled that requirement. The next challenge was to solve the absorption problem. Coconut flour soaks up liquid like a dry sponge. In order to get the consistency you would from wheat flour, you need to add a great deal of liquid, but when the bread is cooked, the high moisture content completely alters cooking time and the texture of the product. So liquids were kept at a bare minimum. To keep the

Delicious cakes and other baked goods can be made using 100 percnet coconut flour.

bread from becoming too dry, oil, usually butter or coconut oil were added. Oil keeps the product moist and soft. The results were incredible! I was able to make delicious tasting breads, cakes, and desserts of all types that were every bit as good as those made with wheat flour. They were light, fluffy, and moist. People couldn't tell they were made from coconut flour instead of wheat.

I had discovered the secret to using 100 percent coconut flour to make quality-baked goods. These products taste as good as, if not better, than wheat but without the gluten—and without the high carb and calorie content. Although the foods in this book such as blueberry muffins, cherry pie, and German chocolate cake are familiar to almost everyone, the recipes are all original. Every recipe in this book was developed through a process of trial and error. This book is the only source for 100 percent coconut flour recipes.

Coconut Flour Tips

Because coconut flour has a high capacity to absorb moisture, it is best to keep it stored in an airtight container. If left open, the flour will absorb moisture from the air, causing it to form lumps and spoil more rapidly. If you live in a climate that has high humidity, you need to pay particular attention to storing the flour properly.

After being opened, coconut flour—when stored at room temperature—will remain fresh for several months. If refrigerated it will last 6 months to a year; frozen it will stay fresh well over two years. I've used flour that has been frozen for over two years and have not detected any changes in flavor. If kept unopened and frozen, the flour should remain usable for years.

Coconut flour naturally tends to form clumps. Some clumping will be present even before you open the package. This is to be expected and is not a problem. The lumps easily break up. When making most breads with coconut flour, it is recommended that you first sift the flour to allow for even mixing. If a recipe calls for half a cup of coconut flour, measure out the flour first then sift it.

Coconut flour tends to absorb a large amount of liquid. For this reason, the texture of the batter may look different from that made with wheat flour. For some recipes the batter becomes so thick, you might be tempted to add more liquid to thin it out. However, instead of making the batter thinner, adding more liquid only makes it thicker, the opposite of what you would expect. Adding more liquid will not thin it out. If you keep adding liquid, it will reach a saturation point and become thinner; however, when you cook the batter, it will not produce good results. If you want to thin the batter, you can generally do so by adding a little coconut milk or more oil.

For some of the recipes the batter may seem too runny, that's okay. When cooked, the batter will firm up and produce good results.

Substitutions

I recommend that you follow the recipes exactly as given. A few substitutions, however, can be made without adversely affecting the final product. In most cases, coconut oil and butter can be used interchangeably. The primary exception is with cookies; be sure to use butter wherever it is indicated.

Many recipes will indicate that you can use either butter or coconut oil. In recipes that list only butter, it is best not to substitute. Butter gives some baked goods the best flavor. If desired you may use a half and half mixture of butter and coconut oil.

Some recipes call for the use of coconut milk. These recipes work best with coconut milk or coconut cream, but in general, whole milk or cream will also work.

When a recipe calls for sugar, almost any type of granulated sweetener will work. If a recipe uses honey, you may use any liquid sweetener such as maple syrup or rice syrup. Some sweeteners are sweeter than others. When you make a substitution with sweeteners, keep in mind that the sweetness of the final product may be affected.

Avoid the urge to thicken the batter by adding more coconut flour. Adding more flour may produce an overly dry and crumbly product. Generally, if you allow the batter to sit and rest for a few minutes, it will thicken slightly as the fiber absorbs moisture.

Another interesting characteristic of coconut flour is that if you reduce the sugar content in a recipe, the batter will often become drier and stiffer. This is just the opposite of what you might expect. You would think that reducing the sugar, a dry ingredient, would make the batter more liquidly, but that is not always the case. So if you reduce the sugar called for in a recipe, you may also need to add a little more liquid, coconut milk or whole milk, to maintain consistency.

Sugar is an important ingredient in many of the recipes because it greatly affects both the taste and texture of the product. Reducing the amount of sugar called for may significantly affect the outcome of the product. I have provided many reduced sugar recipes to give you guidance. Adding more sugar is usually not a problem. If you want to sweeten a recipe, you can generally add more sugar without adversely affecting the texture.

All the recipes in this book have been carefully designed and tested. Changing the recipes in any way may produce inferior results. Do not make substitutions other than those indicated, and do *not approximate* the measurements. Even a very slight deviation from the recipes could have a significant impact on the final outcome. Measure each ingredient exactly as given using measuring spoons and cups. Do not use serving spoons or dinnerware for measuring. As you become more familiar with using coconut flour and learn of its unique characteristics, you can begin to experiment and make adjustments.

INGREDIENTS USED IN THIS BOOK
Fats and Oils
Most of the recipes in this book call for the use of oil either as an ingredient or to lubricate pans and bakeware. As an ingredient, I generally recommend using coconut oil or butter. Both are heat stable and give the foods added flavor. Do not omit the oil from the recipes. Oil makes the bread soft and moist, improving its taste and texture.

Bakeware and skillets often need a coating of oil to prevent sticking. Coconut oil or butter can be used for this purpose as can palm oil or lard if you desire. For pan frying, any of these oils can be used. Butter tends to burn easily and must be limited to moderate temperatures and carefully watched. Lard has the highest smoke point and has the best anti-sticking character of all these oils. Coconut oil has modest anti-sticking ability but generally you need to use a generous amount to prevent sticking.

For baking, the absolute best anti-sticking oil you can use is a combination of coconut oil and liquid lecithin. Use the oil to coat baking dishes and bread pans. All that is needed is a *thin* layer to do the job. Store the remainder in the refrigerator. The coconut oil-lecithin combination is so effective, bread almost pops out of the pan. Clean up is a breeze as well: no sticking or burning so pans easily wipe clean. No scrubbing or harsh cleansing pads needed. Once you begin to use this oil, you won't want to use any other in your baking ever again. Finding the ingredients and mixing them in the right proportions is a nuisance for most people so I have made arrangements with a company to prepare this oil commercially. For lack of a better name I call it Dr. Fife's Non-Stick Cooking Oil. Look for it at your local health food store. If they don't carry it ask them to order it. If you can't find it in any of your local stores you can get it by mail. See page 151 for details.

To give you an example of how effective this oil is, let me tell you about an experience I had with it. I set the oven to 400 degrees F (205 C) and planned to bake muffins for 15 minutes. As they were cooking, I became involved in something else and completely forgot about them until 2½ hours later. You can imagine what they must have looked like after cooking all this time. When I remembered the muffins, I ran into the kitchen and was greeted by a cloud of smoke bellowing out of the oven. The muffins were completely burned to a crisp. They resembled little lumps of black charcoal. Ordinarily food that is burned onto a pan like this is a nightmare to clean, almost requiring a hammer and chisel to break loose. In the past, I've thrown away pans rather than struggle with trying to clean off burned residue. Because I used my Non-Stick Cooking Oil, the charcoal muffins popped right out without difficulty, and with almost no burnt or incrusted batter on the pan. What little was clinging to the pan wiped off easily with a wet washcloth. I was amazed! I now use this oil for all of my baking. By the way, coconut charcoal is not one of my most popular recipes so you won't find it in this book.

My oil mixture is used only to coat bakeware; it is not used as an ingredient in bread making or pan frying. I generally recommend *pure* coconut oil for frying or as an ingredient in foods.

Coconut oil is versatile; it can be used in just about any recipe that calls for vegetable oil, shortening, butter, or margarine. Coconut oil is excellent for cooking. Unlike other vegetable oils, it is very stable when heated and does not create toxic byproducts. You can feel safe when you eat it, knowing that you aren't damaging your health. Coconut oil, however, has a moderate smoking point when used for frying, so you need to keep the temperature under 350 degrees F (175 C). If you don't have a temperature gauge on your stove, you can tell when it goes over this point because the oil will begin to smoke. This is a moderate temperature, but you can cook anything at this heat, even stir-fry vegetables. When coconut oil is used to grease pans or in baked goods, it can be cooked in the oven at higher temperatures because evaporation of water in the food keeps the temperature of both the food and the oil lower.

Because coconut oil is very stable, it does not need to be refrigerated. It will remain good for two or three years unrefrigerated. If kept in a cool place, it will last even longer. It is an excellent storage oil. I buy it by the gallon so that I always have an ample supply on hand.

Coconut oil melts at 76 degrees F (25 C), becoming a clear liquid that looks like almost any other vegetable oil. Below this temperature, it solidifies and takes on a creamy white appearance. At moderate room temperatures it has a soft buttery texture and is sometimes called coconut butter. If your kitchen is cooler than 76 degrees F, the oil will solidify. There is nothing wrong with this. Some people like to store the oil in the refrigerator. To liquefy the hardened oil, simply immerse the bottom of the jar in hot water for a few minutes. The oil melts quickly.

When using coconut oil and even coconut milk in recipes, you need to have all ingredients at room temperature before starting. Coconut oil must be melted, but not hot. Coconut milk, as well, should be warm or at least at room temperature. Eggs should be at room temperature too. It is best that all ingredients be at or near room temperature. If ingredients are too cold, when they are combined, the coconut oil and even the oil in the coconut milk will harden and form unwanted lumps. On a cold day you may need to warm eggs in a pan of hot water before using them.

Numerous processes are used to produce coconut oil, and the quality and taste of the oil varies from brand to brand. Two of the most popular types of coconut oil are virgin and expeller pressed. Virgin coconut oil has had minimal processing and retains a mild coconut taste and aroma. Expeller pressed coconut oil has undergone more processing and is essentially flavorless and odorless. Either oil can be used for any type of cooking or food preparation. Virgin coconut oil is preferred if you want to give foods a hint of coconut flavor. Its flavor is generally so mild that even moderately flavored foods will completely mask the coconut taste. For people who prefer not to have the coconut flavor in their food, expeller pressed oil is generally preferred.

Many of the recipes in this book use butter. Sometimes coconut oil and butter can be used interchangeably. For flavor, real butter is hard to beat. I don't recommend margarine because it contains health damaging trans fatty acids. Butter gives baked goods a delightful buttery taste, enhancing the flavor of the product. In some cases butter is preferred not only for the taste but also for the texture and appearance.

Sugar and Sweeteners
Many of the recipes in this book call for sweeteners. I prefer to use the least processed sweeteners I can find because I believe them to be healthier, or at least less harmful, than highly refined or artificial sweeteners. No artificial sweeteners or sugar substitutes are used in any of the recipes in this book.

I prefer to use sucanat, which is dried sugarcane juice, over most other sweeteners. Muscavado (unprocessed sugar), date sugar, palm sugar, or dehydrated maple syrup are other minimally processed sweeteners you can use if you prefer. Of course, if you want to use ordinary white sugar you can. The recipes in this book can be made with any of these. Even with the use of sugar, because coconut flour is mostly non-caloric fiber, the total effective carbohydrate content of the breads are much lower than wheat bread products.

Most of the recipes for sweet breads and desserts in this book include both full sugar and reduced sugar versions. So you can choose the one you prefer. Some of the reduced sugar recipes use no added sugar, relying only on fruit and/or stevia.

Stevia extract is a natural, sweetener derived from a South American herb. It is essentially calorie free. It is about 200 times sweeter than table sugar, so only a little bit is needed to achieve the same level of sweetness. Stevia extract is available as both a powder and as a liquid. The major drawback with stevia is that if you use too much, it produces a bitter aftertaste. For most recipes, you cannot replace *all* of the sugar with stevia. For best results, you need to combine stevia with other sweeteners or with fruit. This way, you can significantly reduce the total amount of sugar called for in many recipes. For example, you can reduce the sugar content in a recipe by half if you replace the other half with a little stevia. You will still achieve a sweet taste but with only half the sugar.

If the recipe includes fruit, you can often eliminate all the sugar and use stevia instead. The fruit provides just enough natural sweetening to complement the stevia so that together they provide all the sweetness necessary.

You may add more or less stevia to the recipes in this book to suit your taste. When you substitute stevia for sugar, be careful not to use too much. A little can go a long way and too much can give the food an overpowering aftertaste. If you are not accustomed to using stevia, it may take a little practice to find just the right amount to use to suit your taste. Stevia extract is available at most health food stores.

Coconut Meat and Milk

Dried coconut meat is sold as desiccated or flaked coconut. Dried coconut, naturally, has all the health benefits of coconut flour. Many of the recipes in this book call for the use of flaked coconut. When flaked coconut is called for in a recipe, it means "unsweetened" dried coconut. Most dried coconut sold in grocery stores is sweetened, so look on the label to make sure no sugar has been added. Health food stores carry unsweetened coconut.

Coconut milk is another product that is used in many of the recipes. Contrary to popular belief, the liquid inside a fresh coconut is *not* coconut milk. This liquid is known as coconut water or coconut juice. Coconut milk is manufactured by squeezing or extracting the liquid from coconut meat. The two are very different in taste and appearance.

Coconut milk has a milky white color, creamy texture, and nutty flavor. Canned coconut milk is available in most grocery and health food stores. It is most commonly sold in 14-ounce cans but is also available in larger cans as well as cartons. In addition to coconut milk, you can also find coconut cream, which has a slightly higher fat content. Don't confuse coconut milk or coconut cream with *cream of coconut*. Cream of coconut is coconut cream *with sugar added* and is very sweet. It is often used in beverages and desserts. The recipes in this book use *unsweetened* coconut milk. If in doubt whether a brand of milk or cream has been sweetened, look at the ingredient label.

Some coconut milks have been watered down to reduce the fat content. This is called "low-fat" or "lite" coconut milk. To retain the milk's thick texture, thickeners such as guar gum are added. I usually avoid low-fat milks because the coconut oil content is reduced, and the natural higher fat content works better in the recipes.

When canned coconut milk sits on a shelf for any length of time, the cream often separates and floats to the top, particularly with brands that do not add thickeners. To mix the cream, simply shake the can vigorously before opening.

Coconut milk spoils quickly after it has been opened. When stored in an airtight container in the refrigerator, it will last for about four days. If frozen, it will last for six months or longer.

Flours

Most of the recipes in this book use only coconut flour. A few recipes include other flours such as cornmeal, cornstarch, arrowroot, or almond flour. Cornmeal is used in a few recipes such as the Corn Bread Muffins, which traditionally uses cornmeal and is a characteristic of the bread. Cornstarch and arrowroot are used in a few recipes as thickeners. Although coconut flour absorbs liquids readily, it does not make a good thickener for gravies and sauces. Almond flour is used to make some of the cookies and piecrusts. Almonds have a nice flavor and the coconut-almond combination goes very well together. Almond flour is available at health food stores.

One of the biggest drawbacks to every gluten-free recipe book I have seen is the need to use a half dozen different flours along with stabilizers, dough enhancers, gums, and other ingredients in almost every recipe. To make a simple muffin you need a dozen ingredients. With coconut flour you don't need any additional flours. Coconut flour, eggs, and oil: those are the basic ingredients for most all of the recipes in this book.

As you begin to use coconut flour and experiment with it, you may develop some of your own recipes with excellent results. I would like to know about your success with coconut flour. I'm always looking for new coconut flour recipes that I can share with others. Please feel free to write to me and share your experiences and recipes or to make comments about the recipes in this book. Your input is appreciated. You can contact me through the publisher of this book at Piccadilly Books, Ltd., P.O. Box 25203, Colorado Springs, CO 80936, USA or by e-mail at info@piccadillybooks.com.

To learn more about the health benefits of coconut flour, coconut oil, and other coconut products visit my Web site at www.coconutresearchcenter.org.

2
≈≈

Quick Breads

This chapter contains recipes for a variety of quick breads such as pancakes, biscuits, and pumpkin bread. Coconut flour is the only or the primary flour used in most of these recipes though a few other flours are used to make specialty breads such as cornbread. Occasionally cornstarch is added to improve texture, but most recipes rely on 100 percent coconut flour. Baking powder or eggs are the only leavening used.

For those recipes that require baking, I recommend that you use Dr. Fife's Non-Stick Cooking Oil (see page 37). This is absolutely the best oil you can use to prevent sticking. It also makes cleanup a breeze. Use it to coat any pan or cookie sheet used in the oven. A thin coat is all you need. For frying, use ghee, coconut oil, or palm oil. You can also use butter, but it has a lower smoke point so you need to cook at a lower temperature and keep a careful eye on it to avoid burning.

COCONUT BREAD

This is an unsweetened bread that can be eaten much like regular bread. You can serve it plain or with butter, jam, peanut butter, sliced meat, or most any other accompaniment. Unlike wheat breads, this recipe does not use yeast. Leavening comes from eggs and baking powder. Since coconut flour lacks gluten, it does not hold together as firmly as regular bread. So its texture and appearance are different from wheat based breads. This recipe makes one small loaf.

6 eggs
½ cup butter, melted
2 tablespoons honey
½ teaspoon salt
¾ cup sifted coconut flour
1 teaspoon baking powder

Blend together eggs, butter, honey, and salt. Combine coconut flour with baking powder and whisk thoroughly into batter until there are no lumps. Pour into greased 9x5x3-inch or smaller loaf pan and bake at 350 degrees F (175 C) for 40 minutes. Remove from pan and cool on rack.

PANCAKES

2 eggs
2 tablespoons coconut oil or butter, melted
2 tablespoons coconut milk or whole milk
1 teaspoon sugar
⅛ teaspoon salt
2 tablespoons sifted coconut flour
⅛ teaspoon baking powder

Blend together eggs, oil, coconut milk, sugar, and salt. Combine coconut flour and baking powder and thoroughly mix into batter. Heat 1 tablespoon of coconut oil in a skillet. Spoon batter onto hot skillet making pancakes about 2½ to 3 inches in diameter. Batter will be thick but will flatten out when cooking. Makes about 8 pancakes.

Pecan Pancakes
Make Pancakes as directed above and add ½ cup of chopped pecans.

Blueberry Pancakes
Make Pancakes as directed and, after mixing in the coconut milk, fold in ½ cup of dry fresh blueberries.

COCONUT MILK PANCAKES

2 eggs
2 tablespoons coconut oil or butter, melted
¼ teaspoon coconut extract or vanilla
⅓ cup coconut milk
1 teaspoon sugar
⅛ teaspoon salt
3 tablespoons sifted coconut flour
⅛ teaspoon baking powder

Blend together eggs, oil, coconut extract or vanilla, coconut milk, sugar, and salt. Combine coconut flour with baking powder and thoroughly mix into batter. Heat 1 tablespoon of coconut oil in a skillet. Spoon batter onto hot skillet making pancakes about 2½ to 3 inches in diameter. Makes 8 to 10 pancakes.

CREPES

2 eggs
2 tablespoons coconut oil or butter, melted
1 teaspoon sugar
⅛ teaspoon salt
2 tablespoons sifted coconut flour
⅓ cup coconut milk

Blend together eggs, oil, sugar, and salt. Thoroughly mix in coconut flour. Stir in coconut milk. Heat 1 tablespoon of coconut oil in a small skillet. Pour a fourth of the batter into the skillet; immediately rotate skillet until a thin even layer of batter covers the bottom of the skillet. Crepe should be about 5 to 6 inches in diameter. Cook until batter is bubbly and cooked around the edges. Turn and cook other side. Cover one side of crepes with your choice of chopped fruit, nuts, or jelly. Roll up and sprinkle with powdered sugar or top with whipped cream. Makes 4 crepes.

DROP BISCUITS

4 eggs
¼ cup butter or coconut oil, melted
¼ cup honey
¼ teaspoon salt
⅓ cup sifted coconut flour
¼ teaspoon baking powder

Blend together eggs, butter, honey, and salt. Combine coconut flour with baking powder and whisk into batter until there are no lumps remaining. Drop batter by the spoonful onto greased cookie sheet. Bake at 400 degrees F (205 C) for 14 to 15 minutes. Makes 8 biscuits.

CHEESE BISCUITS

4 eggs
¼ cup butter or coconut oil, melted
¼ teaspoon salt
¼ teaspoon onion powder
⅓ cup sifted coconut flour
¼ teaspoon baking powder
½ cup sharp cheddar cheese, shredded

Blend together eggs, butter, salt, and onion powder. Combine coconut flour with baking powder and whisk into batter until there are no lumps. Fold in cheese. Drop batter by the spoonful onto greased cookie sheet. Bake at 400 degrees F (205 C) for 15 minutes. Makes 8 biscuits. For a cheesier biscuit increase cheese to ¾ cup.

Garlic Cheese Biscuits
Make Cheese Biscuits as directed and fold into batter 8 diced cloves of garlic.

BACON BISCUITS

4 eggs
¼ cup bacon drippings
¼ teaspoon salt
⅓ cup sifted coconut flour
¼ teaspoon baking powder
6 to 8 strips crisp bacon, crumbled

Blend together eggs, bacon drippings, and salt. Combine coconut flour with baking powder and whisk into batter until there are no lumps remaining. Fold bacon into batter. Drop batter by the spoonful onto greased cookie sheet. Bake at 400 degrees F (205 C) for 14 to 15 minutes. Makes 8 biscuits.

CORN BREAD

6 eggs
⅓ cup butter or coconut oil, melted
⅓ cup honey
½ teaspoon vanilla
½ teaspoon salt
¼ cup sifted coconut flour
½ teaspoon baking powder
⅓ cup cornmeal

Blend together eggs, butter, honey, vanilla, and salt. Combine coconut flour, baking powder, and cornmeal and whisk into batter until there are no lumps. Fill greased 8x8x2-inch baking dish. Bake at 400 degrees F (205 C) for 15-18 minutes. Makes 8 servings.

Cinnamon Corn Bread
Make Cornbread as directed but omit the honey and add ½ cup sucanat or sugar and 1 tablespoon cinnamon. Sprinkle extra cinnamon on top of batter just before baking.

TEXAS CORN BREAD

6 eggs
⅓ cup butter or coconut oil, melted
1 tablespoon sugar (optional)
1 teaspoon onion powder
1 teaspoon salt

¼ cup sifted coconut flour
½ teaspoon baking powder
⅓ cup cornmeal
¼ cup onion, diced
¼ cup bell pepper, diced
½ cup corn
1 cup sharp cheddar cheese, shredded

Blend together eggs, butter, sugar, onion powder, and salt. Combine coconut flour, baking powder, and cornmeal and whisk into batter until there are no lumps. Fold in onion, bell pepper, corn, and cheese. Pour into a greased 8x8x2-inch baking dish. Bake at 400 degrees F (205 C) for 15-18 minutes. Makes 10 servings.

Jalapeno Corn Bread
Make Texas Cornbread as directed but replace the bell pepper with jalapeno pepper.

POPOVERS

Popovers are simply Yorkshire pudding batter cooked in muffin cups. Traditionally popovers are made using white flour and milk. This recipe replaces those ingredients with coconut flour and coconut milk and adds a bit of cornstarch. The results are just as tasty as the original. Popovers usually accompany a roast and are best when served hot, right out of the oven and smothered with gravy. Makes a great alternative to mashed potatoes.

4 eggs
½ cup coconut milk
¼ teaspoon salt
2 tablespoons sifted coconut flour
3 tablespoons corn starch

With an electric blender or whisk, blend together all ingredients until there are no lumps and batter is slightly bubbly. Fill greased muffin cups two-thirds. Bake at 425 degrees F (225 C) for 20 minutes without opening oven door. Popovers will expand while cooking until they almost seem to pop over sideways. Makes 6 popovers. These popovers are best when served hot, immediately after removing from the oven.

YORKSHIRE PUDDING

Traditionally, Yorkshire pudding is cooked in a pan and served cut into large squares. This is the traditional method. Serve with roast beef and smother in gravy.

4 eggs
½ cup coconut milk
¼ teaspoon salt
2 tablespoons sifted coconut flour
3 tablespoons corn starch

With an electric blender or hand held whisk, blend together all ingredients until there are no lumps and batter is slightly bubbly. Pour batter into a greased 11x7x2-inch baking pan. Bake at 425 degrees F (225 C) for 25 minutes. Remove from oven, cut into 6 equal-sized pieces, and serve immediately.

BANANA NUT BREAD

1 ripe banana, mashed
8 eggs
½ cup coconut milk
½ cup sucanat or brown sugar
½ teaspoon vanilla
½ teaspoon almond extract
½ teaspoon salt
¾ cup sifted coconut flour

1 teaspoon baking powder
½ cup pecans or walnuts, chopped

Blend together mashed banana, eggs, coconut milk, sugar, vanilla, almond extract, and salt. Combine coconut flour with baking powder and whisk thoroughly into batter until there are no lumps. Fold in nuts. Pour into greased 9x5x3-inch loaf pan and bake at 350 degrees F (175 C) for 60 minutes. Remove from pan and cool on rack.

Reduced Sugar Banana Nut Bread
Make Banana Nut Bread as directed but reduce the sugar to ¼ cup and add 1½ teaspoons liquid stevia.

HAWAIIAN NUT BREAD

1 ripe banana, mashed
¼ cup crushed pineapple
8 eggs
½ cup honey
1½ teaspoons lemon extract
½ teaspoon salt
¾ cup sifted coconut flour
1 teaspoon baking powder
¼ cup flaked coconut
½ cup macadamia nuts or pecans, finely chopped

Blend together mashed banana, pineapple, eggs, honey, lemon extract, and salt. Combine coconut flour with baking powder and whisk thoroughly into batter. Fold in nuts. Pour into greased 9x5x3-inch loaf pan and bake at 350 degrees F (175 C) for 55 to 60 minutes. Remove from pan and cool on rack.

Reduced Sugar Hawaiian Nut Bread
Make Hawaiian Nut Bread as directed but reduce honey to ¼ cup and add ½ teaspoon liquid stevia.

PUMPKIN BREAD

½ cup canned pumpkin
8 eggs
½ cup coconut oil or butter, melted
½ cup sucanat or brown sugar
1 teaspoon vanilla
1½ teaspoons ground cinnamon
½ teaspoon ground mace
½ teaspoon salt
¾ cup sifted coconut flour
1 teaspoon baking powder
½ cup pecans or walnuts, chopped

Blend together pumpkin, eggs, oil, sugar, vanilla, cinnamon, mace, and salt. Combine coconut flour with baking powder and whisk thoroughly into batter until there are no lumps. Fold in nuts. Pour into greased 9x5x3-inch loaf pan and bake at 350 degrees F (175 C) for 60 minutes. Remove from pan and cool on rack.

Reduced Sugar Pumpkin Bread
Make Pumpkin Bread as directed but reduce sugar to ¼ cup and add 1½ teaspoons liquid stevia.

Zucchini Bread
Make Pumpkin Bread as directed but omit the pumpkin and add ¾ cup loosely packed, shredded zucchini.

GINGERBREAD

8 eggs
½ cup coconut oil or butter, melted
½ cup coconut milk or whole milk
¼ cup molasses
½ cup sugar
1 teaspoon vanilla

1 teaspoon ground ginger
1 teaspoon ground cinnamon
¼ teaspoon ground cloves
½ teaspoon salt
⅔ cup sifted coconut flour
1 teaspoon baking powder

Blend together eggs, oil, coconut milk, sugar, vanilla, ginger, cinnamon, and salt. Combine coconut flour with baking powder and whisk thoroughly into batter until there are no lumps. Batter will be runny. Pour into greased 9x5x3-inch loaf pan and bake at 350 degrees F (175 C) for 55 to 60 minutes. Remove from pan and cool on rack.

Reduced Sugar Gingerbread
Make Gingerbread as directed but replace the sugar with 1 teaspoon liquid stevia. Do not omit the molasses.

CRANBERRY WALNUT BREAD

8 eggs
½ cup coconut oil or butter, melted
½ cup coconut milk
½ cup sucanat or sugar
1 teaspoon vanilla
1 teaspoon lemon extract
½ teaspoon salt
⅔ cup sifted coconut flour
1 teaspoon baking powder
1 cup dried cranberries
½ cup walnuts, chopped

Blend together eggs, oil, coconut milk, sugar, vanilla, lemon extract, and salt. Combine coconut flour with baking powder and whisk thoroughly into batter until there are no lumps. Fold in cranberry sauce and nuts. Pour into greased 9x5x3-inch loaf pan and bake at 350 degrees F (175 C) for 60 minutes. Remove from pan and cool on rack.

Reduced Sugar Cranberry Walnut Bread

Make Cranberry Walnut Bread as directed but replace the sugar with 1 teaspoon liquid stevia (about 50 drops).

3

Muffins

Coconut flour makes fantastic muffins. They are quick and easy to make and taste terrific. There are so many different types of muffins that you can make with coconut flour that an entire chapter is needed to do it justice. You will find recipes for sweet muffins, such as Blueberry Muffins, Apple Cinnamon Muffins, Banana Nut Muffins, and even some unusual ones such Pina Colada Muffins and Peanut Butter Muffins (one of my favorites). If you're concerned about the carbohydrate or sugar content, each of the sweet muffin recipes also has a reduced sugar version. The No Sugar Muffin recipe contains almost no digestible carbohydrate and tastes as good as any ordinary muffin. You will also find savory muffins such as Bacon Muffins, Broccoli Cheese Muffins, and Ham and Cheese Muffins. The muffins in this chapter are perfect for breakfast, make a great accompaniment for lunch or dinner, or a tasty snack at anytime of the day.

Muffin pans need to be greased before adding the batter to prevent sticking and burning. My Non-Stick Cooking Oil is by far the best oil you can use for this purpose. Muffins almost pop out of the cups without any effort. A thin layer of oil is all that is needed to do the job. No burnt or crusty residue is left in the cups, so cleanup is a breeze. If you don't have this oil available, you can use a generous amount of butter.

Baking Tips
- Bring all ingredients to room temperature before mixing. Coconut oil should be melted but not hot.
- Dr. Fife's Non-Stick Cooking Oil is the best oil to use for baking.
- In most bread recipes you can substitute coconut milk for coconut oil and vice versa.
- Muffins taste best when served warm right out of the oven.

HONEY MUFFINS

This is a basic coconut flour muffin recipe you can use to make a variety of muffins.

3 eggs
2 tablespoons butter, melted
2 tablespoons coconut milk or whole milk
3 tablespoons honey
¼ teaspoon salt
¼ teaspoon vanilla
¼ cup sifted coconut flour
¼ teaspoon baking powder

Blend together eggs, butter, coconut milk, honey, salt, and vanilla. Combine coconut flour with baking powder and thoroughly mix into batter until there are no lumps. Pour batter into greased muffin cups. Bake at 400 degrees F (205 C) for 15 minutes. Makes 6 muffins.

Honey Nut Muffins
Make Honey Muffins as directed and add ½ cup of chopped pecans and ⅛ teaspoon almond extract.

Lemon Poppy Seed Muffins
Make Honey Muffins as directed but omit the vanilla and add 2 teaspoons of lemon extract. Sprinkle poppy seeds on top of muffins just before baking.

Cherry Muffins
Make Honey Muffins as directed and add ½ cup dried cherries and ⅛ teaspoon almond extract.

Prune Nut Muffins
Make Honey Muffins as directed and add ½ cup chopped prunes and ¼ cup chopped nuts.

Apricot Muffins
Make Honey Muffins as directed and add ½ cup dried apricots and ⅛ teaspoon almond extract.

BLUEBERRY MUFFINS

3 eggs
3 tablespoons butter, melted
3 tablespoons honey
¼ teaspoon salt
¼ teaspoon vanilla
⅛ teaspoon almond extract
¼ cup sifted coconut flour
¼ teaspoon baking powder
½ cup fresh blueberries

Blend together eggs, butter, honey, salt, and vanilla. Combine coconut flour with baking powder and thoroughly mix into batter until there are no lumps. Fold blueberries into batter. Blueberries should be dry. If rinsed, dry them off before adding to batter. Pour batter into greased muffin cups. Bake at 400 degrees F (205 C) for 16-18 minutes. Makes 6 muffins.

Raspberry Muffins

Make Blueberry Muffins as directed but omit the blueberries and add ½ cup of fresh raspberries. Raspberries should be dry. If rinsed, dry them off before adding to batter.

Apple Nut Muffins

Make Blueberry Muffins as directed but omit the blueberries and add ½ cup finely chopped tart apple, ¼ teaspoon ground cinnamon, and ¼ cup chopped walnuts or pecans.

NO SUGAR MUFFINS

Here is a muffin recipe that contains no sugar. Sweetness comes from stevia.

3 eggs
2 tablespoons butter, melted
2 tablespoons coconut milk

30 drops liquid stevia
¼ teaspoon salt
¼ teaspoon vanilla
¼ cup sifted coconut flour
¼ teaspoon baking powder

Blend together eggs, butter, coconut milk, stevia, salt, and vanilla. Combine coconut flour with baking powder and thoroughly mix into batter until there are no lumps. Pour batter into greased muffin cups. Bake at 400 degrees F (205 C) for 15 minutes. Makes 6 muffins.

No Sugar Bluberry Muffins
Make No Sugar Muffins as directed and add ½ cup blueberries. Fruit should be dry. If rinsed, dry the fruit before adding to the batter. Increase baking time to 16-18 minutes.

No Sugar Nut Muffins
Make No Sugar Honey Muffins as directed and add ½ cup of chopped nuts and ⅛ teaspoon almond extract.

No Sugar Lemon Poppy Seed Muffins
Make No Sugar Honey Muffins as directed but omit the vanilla and add 2 teaspoons of lemon extract. Sprinkle poppy seeds on top of muffins just before baking.

COCONUT MUFFINS

3 eggs
2 tablespoons butter or coconut oil, melted
⅓ cup sucanat or sugar
¼ teaspoon salt
½ teaspoon coconut extract
¼ cup sifted coconut flour
¼ teaspoon baking powder
3 tablespoons flaked coconut

Blend together eggs, butter, sugar, salt, and coconut extract. Combine coconut flour with baking powder and whisk into batter until there are no lumps. Pour batter into greased muffin cups. Sprinkle grated coconut on top. Bake at 400 degrees F (205 C) for 15 minutes. Makes 6 muffins.

Reduced Sugar Coconut Muffins
Make Coconut Muffins as directed but omit sugar and add 30 drops of liquid stevia.

COCONUT MILK MUFFINS

3 eggs
¼ cup coconut milk
3 teaspoons sucanat or brown sugar
¼ teaspoon salt
¼ cup sifted coconut flour
¼ teaspoon baking powder
¼ cup flaked coconut

Blend together eggs, coconut milk, sugar, and salt. Combine coconut flour with baking powder and whisk into batter until there are no lumps. Pour batter into greased muffin cups. Sprinkle flaked coconut on top. Bake at 400 degrees F (205 C) for 15 minutes. Makes 6 muffins.

Reduced Sugar Coconut Milk Muffins
Make Coconut Milk Muffins as directed but omit sugar and add 30 drops of liquid stevia.

ORANGE MUFFINS

3 eggs
2 tablespoons orange juice concentrate, no water added
2 tablespoons coconut milk
3 tablespoons honey
¼ teaspoon salt

⅛ teaspoon almond extract
¼ cup sifted coconut flour
¼ teaspoon baking powder
2 teaspoons orange peel, finely diced

Blend together eggs, orange juice concentrate, coconut milk, honey, salt, and almond extract. Combine coconut flour with baking powder and whisk into batter until there are no lumps. Fold in orange peel. Pour batter into greased muffin cups. Bake at 400 degrees F (205 C) for 18-20 minutes. Makes 6 muffins.

Reduced Sugar Orange Muffins
Make Orange Muffins as directed but reduce honey to 1 tablespoon and add 20 drops liquid stevia.

PINA COLADA MUFFINS

3 eggs
2 tablespoons butter or coconut oil, melted
¼ cup sucanat or sugar
¼ teaspoon salt
½ teaspoon coconut extract
¼ cup sifted coconut flour
¼ teaspoon baking powder
½ cup pineapple, finely chopped*
3 tablespoons grated coconut

Blend together eggs, butter, sugar, salt, and coconut extract. Combine coconut flour with baking powder and whisk into batter until there are no lumps. Fold pineapple into batter. Pour batter into greased muffin cups. Sprinkle grated coconut on top. Bake at 400 degrees F (205 C) for 16-18 minutes. Makes 6 muffins.

*You may use crushed pineapple if fully drained.

Reduced Sugar Pina Colada Muffins

Make Pina Colada Muffins as directed but omit sugar and add 30 drops of liquid stevia.

WALNUT RAISIN MUFFINS

3 eggs
2 tablespoons butter, melted
2 tablespoons coconut milk
3 tablespoons honey
¼ teaspoon salt
¼ teaspoon vanilla
¼ cup sifted coconut flour
¼ teaspoon baking powder
⅓ cup raisins
⅓ cup walnuts, chopped

Blend together eggs, butter, coconut milk, honey, salt, and vanilla. Combine coconut flour with baking powder and whisk into batter until there are no lumps. Fold in raisins and walnuts. Pour batter into greased muffin cups. Bake at 400 degrees F (205 C) for 15 minutes. Makes 6 muffins.

Reduced Sugar Walnut Raisin Muffins

Make Walnut Raisin Muffins as directed but omit honey and add 30 drops of liquid stevia.

STREUSEL MUFFINS

These coffee cake like muffins are good for breakfast or as a dessert.

Streusel

½ cup walnuts or pecans, chopped
2 tablespoons sucanat or brown sugar
¼ teaspoon ground cinnamon
1 tablespoon butter, softened

Batter

3 eggs
¼ cup coconut milk
¼ cup honey
¼ teaspoon salt
¼ teaspoon vanilla
¼ cup sifted coconut flour
¼ teaspoon baking powder

To make the streusel, mix together nuts, sugar, cinnamon, and butter and set aside. To make the batter, blend together eggs, coconut milk, honey, salt, and vanilla. Combine coconut flour with baking powder and whisk into batter until there are no lumps. Fill greased muffin cups with batter. Sprinkle streusel on top. Bake at 400 degrees F (205 C) for 15 minutes. Makes 6 muffins.

Reduced Sugar Streusel Muffins

Make the batter as directed above but omit the honey and add 30 drops of liquid stevia. Do not make any changes to the streusel.

BANANA NUT MUFFINS

3 eggs
2 tablespoons butter or coconut oil, melted
½ ripe banana, mashed
3 tablespoons sucanat or brown sugar
¼ teaspoon salt
½ teaspoon vanilla
¼ cup sifted coconut flour
¼ teaspoon baking powder
¼ cup walnuts or pecans, chopped

Blend together eggs, butter, banana, sugar, salt, and vanilla. Combine coconut flour with baking powder and whisk into batter until there are no lumps. Fold in nuts. Pour into greased muffin cups. Bake at 400 degrees F (205 C) for 18 minutes. Makes 6 muffins.

Reduced Sugar Banana Nut Muffins
Make Banana Nut Muffins as directed but omit sugar and add 30 drops of liquid stevia.

Chocolate Chip Banana Muffins
Make Banana Nut Muffins as directed and add ¼ cup of semi-sweet chocolate chips.

CARROT NUT MUFFINS

3 eggs
2 tablespoons butter, melted
3 tablespoons honey
¼ teaspoon salt
¼ teaspoon vanilla
¼ cup sifted coconut flour
¼ teaspoon baking powder
½ cup shredded carrot
¼ cup pecans or walnuts, chopped
¼ cup raisins

Blend together eggs, butter, honey, salt, and vanilla. Combine coconut flour with baking powder and whisk into batter until there are no lumps. Fold in carrot, nuts, and raisins. Fill greased muffin cups with batter. Bake at 400 degrees F (205 C) for 16 minutes. Makes 6 muffins.

Reduced Sugar Carrot Nut Muffins
Make Carrot Nut Muffins as directed but reduce honey to 1 tablespoon and add 20 drops liquid stevia.

PUMPKIN MUFFINS

3 eggs
2 tablespoons butter or coconut oil, melted
¼ cup mashed pumpkin
½ cup sucanat or brown sugar
½ teaspoon ground cinnamon
⅛ teaspoon ground mace
¼ teaspoon salt
½ teaspoon vanilla
¼ cup sifted coconut flour
¼ teaspoon baking powder

Blend together eggs, butter, pumpkin, sugar, cinnamon, mace, salt, and vanilla. Combine coconut flour with baking powder and whisk into batter until there are no lumps. Pour batter into greased muffin cups. Bake at 400 degrees F (205 C) for 18 minutes. Makes 6 muffins.

Reduced Sugar Pumpkin Muffins
Make Pumpkin Muffins as directed but reduce sugar to ¼ cup and add 20 drops of liquid stevia.

PEANUT BUTTER MUFFINS

3 eggs
1 tablespoon coconut oil or butter, melted
5 tablespoons sucanat or brown sugar
¼ cup natural peanut butter
¼ teaspoon salt
¼ teaspoon vanilla
¼ cup sifted coconut flour
¼ teaspoon baking powder

Blend together eggs, oil, sugar, peanut butter, salt, and vanilla. Combine coconut flour with baking powder and whisk into batter until there are no lumps. Pour into greased muffin cups. Bake at 400 degrees F (205 C) for 15 minutes. Makes 6 muffins.

Reduced Sugar Peanut Butter Muffins

Make Peanut Butter Muffins as directed but reduce sugar to 2 tablespoons and add 30 drops liquid stevia.

Chocolate Chip Peanut Butter Muffins

Make Peanut Butter Muffins as directed and mix into batter ¼ cup of sweet milk chocolate chips.

FIBER-RICH COCONUT MUFFINS

3 eggs
2 tablespoons butter or coconut oil, melted
⅓ cup sucanat or sugar
¼ teaspoon salt
¼ teaspoon almond extract
¼ cup sifted coconut flour
¼ teaspoon baking powder
½ cup grated coconut

Blend together eggs, butter, sugar, salt, and almond extract. Combine coconut flour with baking powder and whisk into batter until there are no lumps. Fold in grated coconut. Pour into greased muffin cups. Bake at 400 degrees F (205 C) for 15 minutes. Makes 6 muffins.

Reduced Sugar Fiber-Rich Coconut Muffins

Make Fiber-Rich Coconut Muffins as directed but reduce the sugar to 1 tablespoon and add 30 drops of liquid stevia.

BEST EVER CORN BREAD MUFFINS

3 eggs
3 tablespoons butter or coconut oil, melted

3 tablespoons honey
¼ teaspoon vanilla
¼ teaspoon salt
2 tablespoons sifted coconut flour
¼ teaspoon baking powder
3 tablespoons cornmeal

Blend together eggs, butter, honey, vanilla, and salt. Combine coconut flour, baking powder, and cornmeal and whisk into batter until there are no lumps. Pour batter into greased muffin cups. Bake at 400 degrees F (205 C) for 12 to15 minutes. Makes 6 muffins.

Reduced Sugar Best Ever Corn Bread Muffins
Make Best Ever Cornbread Muffins as directed but omit honey and add 30 drops of liquid stevia and 3 tablespoons coconut milk.

CINNAMON CORN BREAD MUFFINS

3 eggs
3 tablespoons butter or coconut oil, melted
3 tablespoons coconut milk
3 tablespoons sucanat or sugar
¼ teaspoon vanilla
¼ teaspoon salt
2 tablespoons sifted coconut flour
¼ teaspoon baking powder
3 tablespoons cornmeal
1 teaspoon cinnamon

Blend together eggs, butter, coconut milk, 2 tablespoons sugar, vanilla, and salt. Combine coconut flour, baking powder, and cornmeal and whisk into batter until there are no lumps. Pour batter into greased muffin cups. Combine 1 tablespoon sugar with cinnamon and sprinkle on top of batter. Bake at 400 degrees F (205 C) for 12 to15 minutes. Makes 6 muffins.

Reduced Sugar Cinnamon Corn Bread Muffins

Make Cinnamon Cornbread Muffins as directed but omit the sugar from the batter and add 20 drops of liquid stevia. Sprinkle top of batter with combination of 1 tablespoon sugar and 1 teaspoon cinnamon.

CORN BREAD CHEESE MUFFINS

3 eggs
3 tablespoons butter or coconut oil, melted
3 tablespoons coconut milk
¼ teaspoon salt
2 tablespoons sifted coconut flour
¼ teaspoon baking powder
3 tablespoons cornmeal
¾ cup sharp cheddar cheese, shredded

Blend together eggs, butter, coconut milk, and salt. Combine coconut flour, baking powder, and cornmeal and whisk into batter until there are no lumps. Fold in cheese. Pour batter into greased muffin cups. Bake at 400 degrees F (205 C) for 12 to15 minutes. Makes 6 muffins.

BACON MUFFINS

3 eggs
2 tablespoons bacon drippings
¼ teaspoon salt
3 tablespoons sifted coconut flour
¼ teaspoon baking powder
8 strips crisp bacon, crumbled
½ cup sharp cheddar cheese, shredded

Blend together eggs, bacon drippings, and salt. Combine coconut flour and baking powder and whisk into batter until there are no lumps. Fold in bacon. Pour batter into greased muffin cups. Top with cheese. Bake at 400 degrees F (205 C) for 15 minutes. Makes 6 muffins.

SAUSAGE MUFFINS

½ pound ground sausage
3 eggs
2 tablespoons coconut oil, butter, or bacon drippings
½ teaspoon salt
¼ onion powder
3 tablespoons sifted coconut flour
¼ teaspoon baking powder
3 tablespoons salsa
¼ cup sharp cheddar cheese, shredded

Lightly brown sausage and set aside. Blend together eggs, oil, salt, and onion powder. Combine coconut flour and baking powder and whisk into batter until there are no lumps. Fold in salsa and sausage; do not over mix. Fill greased muffin cups with batter. Sprinkle cheese on top of muffins. Bake at 400 degrees F (205 C) for 15 minutes. Makes 6 muffins.

BEEF MUFFINS

½ pound ground beef
½ cup onion, finely chopped
3 eggs
2 tablespoons coconut oil or butter, melted
½ teaspoon salt
⅛ teaspoon pepper
¼ teaspoon paprika
¼ teaspoon ground marjoram
3 tablespoons sifted coconut flour
¼ cup sharp cheddar cheese, shredded

Sauté ground beef and onion until meat is brown and onion is tender; set aside. Blend together eggs, oil, salt, pepper, paprika, and marjoram. Stir in coconut flour until there are no lumps remaining. Fold in meat mixture. Fill greased muffin cups with batter. Sprinkle top of muffins with cheese. Bake at 400 degrees F (205 C) for 15 minutes. Makes 6 muffins.

CHEESE MUFFINS

3 eggs
2 tablespoons butter or coconut oil, melted
3 tablespoons coconut milk
¼ teaspoon salt
⅛ teaspoon garlic powder
¼ teaspoon onion powder
¼ cup sifted coconut flour
1 cup sharp cheddar cheese, shredded

Blend together eggs, butter, coconut milk, salt, garlic powder, and onion powder. Stir in coconut flour until there are no lumps remaining. Fold in ¾ cup cheese. Fill greased muffin cups with batter. Sprinkle tops of muffins with the remaining ¼ cup of cheese. Bake at 400 degrees F (205 C) for 15 minutes. Makes 6 muffins.

BROCCOLI CHEESE MUFFINS

3 eggs
2 tablespoons butter or coconut oil, melted
2 tablespoons coconut milk
½ teaspoon salt
⅛ teaspoon pepper
¼ teaspoon onion powder
3 tablespoons sifted coconut flour
¾ cup broccoli, finely chopped
¾ cup sharp cheddar cheese, shredded

Blend together eggs, butter, coconut milk, salt, pepper, and onion powder. Whisk in coconut flour until there are no lumps remaining. Fold in broccoli and ½ cup cheese. Fill greased muffin cups with batter. Sprinkle tops of muffins with the remaining ¼ cup of cheese. Bake at 400 degrees F (205 C) for 15 minutes. Makes 6 muffins.

SEAFOOD MUFFINS

3 eggs
2 tablespoons coconut oil or butter, melted
½ teaspoon salt
½ teaspoon lemon pepper
¼ teaspoon onion powder
3 tablespoons sifted coconut flour
½ cup sharp cheddar cheese, shredded
½ cup cooked fish (your choice of tuna, salmon, halibut, etc.)

Blend together eggs, oil, salt, lemon pepper, and onion powder. Stir in coconut flour until there are no lumps remaining. Fold in cheese and fish. Fill greased muffin cups with batter. Bake at 400 degrees F (205 C) for 15 minutes. Makes 6 muffins.

SHRIMP COCKTAIL MUFFINS

3 eggs
2 tablespoons coconut oil or butter, melted
½ teaspoon salt
¾ teaspoon lemon pepper
¼ teaspoon onion powder
¼ cup sifted coconut flour
¾ -1 cup cooked shrimp, chopped*
3 tablespoons cocktail sauce

*You may substitute crab or lobster for the shrimp if desired.

Blend together eggs, oil, salt, lemon pepper, and onion powder. Stir in coconut flour until there are no lumps remaining. Fold in shrimp. Pour batter into greased muffin cups; top with ½ tablespoon of cocktail sauce in each cup. Bake at 400 degrees F (205 C) for 20 minutes. Makes 6 muffins.

HAM AND CHEESE MUFFINS

3 eggs
2 tablespoons butter or coconut oil, melted
¼ teaspoon salt
¼ teaspoon onion powder
3 tablespoons sifted coconut flour
½ cup sharp cheddar cheese, shredded
½ cup cooked ham, cubed

Blend together eggs, butter, salt, and onion powder. Stir in coconut flour until there are no lumps remaining. Fold in cheese and ham. Fill greased muffin cups with batter. Bake at 400 degrees F (205 C) for 15 minutes. Makes 6 muffins.

Pineapple Ham Muffins

Make the Ham and Cheese Muffins as directed but add ½ cup of crushed pineapple, well drained. Increase cooking time to 18 minutes.

4

Cookies and Crackers

Coconut flour is very well suited for making cookies. Cooconut flour produces soft, cake-like cookies as well as the more traditional crispy varieties. These recipes have been carefully tested. For best results follow the recipes exactly as given, but if you're the adventurous type, please feel free to experiment and create your own. If you are successful in creating a tasty cookie different from those in this chapter please share it with me. I'm always happy to find new recipes.

Many of the cookie recipes call for the use of a *greased* cookie sheet. These are cookies that normally tend to stick a bit. Without question the best oil to use is Dr. Fife's Non-Stick Cooking Oil (page 37). With a thin layer of this oil on the cookie sheet even the stickiest cookies slide off easily. If the recipe calls for an *ungreased* cookie sheet there is no need to use oil but you still can if you want to make cookie removal simple and easy.

COCONUT BUTTER COOKIES

This is one of my favorite cookie recipes. The cookies are similar to macaroons but with a slight buttery flavor—yum!

½ cup butter
1 cup sugar
4 eggs
½ teaspoon vanilla
½ cup sifted coconut flour
2 cups grated or flaked coconut

Mix together butter, sugar, eggs, and vanilla. Stir in coconut flour and coconut. Drop spoon-size mounds 1-inch apart on a greased cookie sheet. Bake at 375 degrees F (190 C) for 18 to 20 minutes or until golden brown. Remove from cookie sheet immediately and cool on wire rack. Makes about 2 dozen cookies.

Reduced Sugar Coconut Butter Cookies

Make Coconut Butter Cookies as directed but reduce sugar to ½ cup and add ¼ teaspoon of powdered stevia.

Coconut Butterscotch Cookies

Make Coconut Butter Cookies as directed and add 1 cup butterscotch chips.

COCONUT ALMOND COOKIES

½ cup chopped almonds, lightly toasted
½ cup butter
1 cup sugar
¼ teaspoon salt
4 eggs
¾ teaspoon almond extract
½ cup sifted coconut flour
1½ cups grated or flaked coconut

Preheat oven to 350 degrees F (175 C). Put almonds in an oven safe pan and bake for about 8 minutes or until lightly browned. Remove from oven and let cool. Mix together butter, sugar, salt, eggs, and almond extract. Stir in flour, coconut, and toasted almonds. Let batter rest for 4 to 5 minutes to allow it to thicken slightly. Drop batter in spoon-size mounds 1-inch apart on greased cookie sheet. Bake at 375 degrees F (190 C) for 15 minutes or until lightly browned. Cool slightly and remove from cookie sheet. Makes about 2 dozen cookies.

Reduced Sugar Coconut Almond Cookies

Make Coconut Almond Cookies as directed but reduce sugar to 3 tablespoons and add ½ teaspoon of liquid or powdered stevia. There is no need to let the batter rest before putting it on the cookie sheet.

GINGERBREAD COOKIES

6 eggs
⅓ cup butter or coconut oil, melted
¼ teaspoon salt
½ cup molasses

¾ cup sucanat or brown sugar
1 teaspoon ground ginger
1 teaspoon ground cinnamon
¼ teaspoon ground cloves
¾ cup sifted coconut flour

Blend together eggs, butter, salt, molasses, sugar, and spices. Stir in coconut flour and mix thoroughly. Batter will thicken slightly as the flour absorbs moisture. Drop batter by spoonfuls onto greased cookie sheet. Bake at 400 degrees F (205 C) for 12-14 minutes. Makes 32 cookies.

Reduced Sugar Gingerbread Cookies
Make Gingerbread Cookies as directed but omit the sugar and add ½ teaspoon liquid or powdered stevia. Do not omit the molasses.

CHOCOLATE COOKIES

¼ cup butter or coconut oil
⅓ cup cocoa powder
3 eggs
⅓ cup sugar
¼ teaspoon salt
¼ teaspoon vanilla
¼ cup sifted coconut flour

In a saucepan at low heat, melt butter and stir in cocoa powder. Remove from heat and let cool. In a bowl, combine eggs, sugar, salt, and vanilla; stir in cocoa mixture. Whisk coconut flour into batter until there are no lumps. Let batter rest 4 to 5 minutes to allow it to thicken slightly. Drop batter by the spoonful on greased cookie sheet. Bake at 350 degrees F (175 C) for 14 minutes. Makes about 16 cookies.

Reduced Sugar Chocolate Cookies
Make Chocolate Cookies as directed but reduce sugar to 3 tablespoons and add ¾ teaspoon liquid or powdered stevia.

PECAN DELIGHTS

½ cup butter
1 cup sucanat or brown sugar
4 eggs
½ teaspoon vanilla
⅛ teaspoon salt
1½ cups grated or flaked coconut
¾ cup pecans, chopped
1 cup sifted coconut flour

Mix together butter, sugar, eggs, vanilla, salt, coconut, and pecans. Stir in coconut flour. Drop batter in spoon-size mounds 1-inch apart on greased cookie sheet. Bake at 375 degrees F (190 C) for 14 to 15 minutes or until lightly browned. Cool slightly and remove from cookie sheet. Makes about 2 dozen cookies.

Reduced Sugar Pecan Delights

Make Pecan Delights as directed but reduce sugar to ⅓ cup and add ¼ teaspoon liquid or powdered stevia. Drop spoon-size mounds on greased cookie sheet. Flatten mounds slightly before baking.

PEANUT BUTTER COOKIES

For these cookies use natural peanut butter, without hydrogenated oil or added sugar. The oil in natural peanut butter usually separates and rises to the top of the jar if allowed to sit for any extended period of time. Mix this oil into the peanut butter. Do not pour it out. If you do pour it out, replace it with an equal amount of melted coconut oil. Maintaining the original fat content of the peanut butter produces the best results with this recipe.

1 cup natural peanut butter
½ cup peanuts, coarsely chopped (optional)
1½ cups brown sugar or sucanat
4 eggs
½ teaspoon vanilla

½ teaspoon salt
½ cup sifted coconut flour

Mix together peanut butter, peanuts, sugar, eggs, vanilla, and salt. Stir in peanuts and coconut flour. Batter will be runny. Drop by the spoonful 2 inches apart on greased cookie sheet. Bake at 375 degrees F (190 C) for 14 to 15 minutes. Cool slightly and remove from cookie sheet. Makes about 3 dozen cookies.

Reduced Sugar Peanut Butter Cookies

Make Peanut Butter according to directions but reduce sugar to ¾ cup and add ½ teaspoon of powdered stevia.

COCONUT CHOCOLATE CHIP COOKIES

½ cup butter, melted
1 cup sucanat or brown sugar
4 eggs
½ teaspoon vanilla
⅛ teaspoon salt
1½ cups grated or flaked coconut
¾ cup semisweet chocolate chips
1 cup sifted coconut flour

Mix together butter, sugar, eggs, vanilla, and salt. Stir in coconut, chocolate chips, and coconut flour. Drop batter in spoon-size mounds 1-inch apart on greased cookie sheet. Bake at 375 degrees F (190 C) for 14 to 15 minutes. Cool slightly and remove from cookie sheet. Makes about 2 dozen cookies.

Reduced Sugar Coconut Chocolate Chip Cookies

Make Coconut Chocolate Chip Cookies as directed but reduce sugar to ½ cup and add ¼ teaspoon powdered or liquid stevia.

NUTTY CHOCOLATE CHIPPERS

Use natural peanut butter, without hydrogenated oil or added sugar. The oil in natural peanut butter usually separates and rises to the top of the jar if allowed to sit for any length of time. Mix this oil into the peanut butter. Do not pour it out. If you do, replace it with an equal amount of melted coconut oil. Maintaining the original fat content of the peanut butter produces the best results.

½ cup natural peanut butter
1¼ cups brown sugar or sucanat
4 eggs
½ teaspoon vanilla
½ teaspoon salt
2 cups nuts, chopped
1 cup sweet chocolate chips
⅔ cup sifted coconut flour

Mix together peanut butter, sugar, eggs, vanilla, and salt. Stir in nuts, chocolate chips, and coconut flour. Batter will be runny. Drop by the spoonful 2 inches apart on greased cookie sheet. Bake at 375 degrees F (190 C) for 13 to 14 minutes or until lightly browned. Cool slightly and remove from cookie sheet. Makes about 3 dozen cookies.

Reduced Sugar Nutty Chocolate Chippers

Make Nutty Chocolate Chippers according to directions but reduce sugar to ¾ cup and add ½ teaspoon of powdered stevia.

CINNAMON SUGAR COOKIES

4 eggs
¾ cup plus 2 tablespoons sugar
½ teaspoon vanilla
¼ teaspoon salt
½ cup butter, melted
¾ cup sifted coconut flour

2 teaspoons cinnamon
1 tablespoon sugar

Combine eggs, sugar, vanilla, salt, and butter and mix well. Stir in coconut flour. Let batter rest for 5 minutes to allow it to thicken. Combine cinnamon with 1 tablespoon sugar. Form dough into 1½-inch balls and roll in cinnamon mixture, coating thoroughly. Place on cookie sheet 1-inch apart; flatten ball to a diameter of about 2 inches. Bake at 375 degrees F (190 C) for 15 minutes. Makes about 2 dozen cookies.

Reduced Sugar Cinnamon Sugar Cookies
Make Cinnamon Sugar Cookies as directed but reduce sugar to ½ cup and add ¼ teaspoon liquid or powdered stevia. Flatten dough on cookie sheet before placing in oven.

LEMON COOKIES

4 eggs
1 cup sugar
1½ teaspoons lemon extract
¼ teaspoon salt
½ cup butter, melted
¾ cup sifted coconut flour

Combine eggs, sugar, lemon extract, salt, and butter and mix well. Stir in coconut flour. Let batter rest for 4-5 minutes to allow it to thicken slightly. Drop batter in spoon-size mounds 2 inches apart on greased cookie sheet. Bake at 375 degrees F (190 C) for 15 minutes. Makes about 2 dozen cookies.

Reduced Sugar Lemon Cookies
Make Lemon Cookies as directed but reduce sugar to ½ cup and add ¼ teaspoon liquid or powdered stevia.

CHOCOLATE ALMOND COCONUT CLUSTERS

½ cup peanut butter
½ cup honey
2 tablespoons coconut oil or butter, softened
¼ teaspoon salt
¼ cup sifted coconut flour
1 cup flaked coconut
1 cup toasted almonds, coarsely chopped
½ cup sweet chocolate chips

Mix peanut butter, honey, coconut oil, and salt together. Stir in coconut flour and mix thoroughly. With your hands, work in flaked coconut, nuts, and chocolate chips. Roll dough into 1½ -inch balls, place on a lightly greased cookie sheet, and flatten balls to a diameter of about 2 inches. Bake at 375 degrees F (190 C) for 12 minutes or until golden brown. When hot, cookies are soft and crumbly so allow them to cool for a few minutes before removing from cookie sheet. Makes about 18 cookies.

Reduced Sugar Chocolate Almond Coconut Clusters
Make the Chocolate Almond Coconut Clusters according to directions but replace honey with gluten-free rice syrup. If more sweetness is desired, add ⅛ teaspoon of liquid or powdered stevia.

FRUIT AND NUT CLUSTERS
This cookie makes an excellent nutty snack. Use a mixture of different types of nuts and seeds. Some suggestions include sesame seeds, pumpkin seeds, sunflower seeds, almonds, pecans, walnuts, and hazelnuts. Virtually any type of nut or seed will work.

½ cup peanut butter*
½ cup honey
¼ cup coconut oil or butter, softened

¼ teaspoon salt
¼ cup plus 2 tablespoons sifted coconut flour
½ cup flaked coconut
1 cup mixed nuts
½ cup raisins or dried fruit

Mix peanut butter, honey, coconut oil, and salt together. Stir in coconut flour and mix thoroughly. With your hands, work in flaked coconut, nuts and raisins. Roll dough into 1½ -inch balls, place on greased cookie sheet, and flatten balls to a diameter of about 2 inches. Bake at 375 degrees F (190 C) for 12 minutes or until golden brown. When hot, cookies are soft and crumbly so allow them to cool for a few minutes before removing from cookie sheet. Makes about 18 cookies.

*In place of peanut butter you may use raw almond butter, cashew butter, or another raw nut butter of your choice. Except for the peanut butter, the nut butter you use must be raw. Roasted nut butters produce a burnt flavor.

Reduced Sugar Fruit and Nut Clusters
Make the Fruit and Nut Clusters according to directions but replace honey with gluten-free rice syrup. If more sweetness is desired, add ⅛ teaspoon of liquid or powdered stevia.

SESAME COCONUT COOKIES
This recipe calls for the use of tahini, which is sesame seed butter. Use raw, not roasted, tahini. If desired, you can use peanut butter or other nut butters in place of the tahini.

½ cup tahini
1 cup honey
1 cup grated or flaked coconut
½ cup sesame seeds
Dash of salt
½ cup sifted coconut flour

Mix the first five ingredients together. Stir in coconut flour. Batter will be sticky. Drop batter by spoonful on greased cookie sheet 2 inches apart. Bake at 350 degrees F (175 C) for 14 minutes or until golden brown. Remove from oven and let cool before removing from cookie sheet.

Reduced Sugar Sesame Coconut Cookies
Make the Sesame Coconut Cookies as directed but replace the honey with ½ cup of gluten-free rice syrup.

BROWNIES

⅓ cup butter or coconut oil
½ cup cocoa powder
6 eggs
1 cup sugar
½ teaspoon salt
½ teaspoon vanilla
½ cup sifted coconut flour
1 cup nuts, chopped (optional)

In a saucepan at low heat, blend together butter and cocoa powder. Remove from heat and let cool. In a bowl, mix together eggs, sugar, salt, and vanilla. Stir in cocoa mixture. Whisk coconut flour into batter until there are no lumps. Fold in nuts. Pour batter into a greased 11x7x2-inch or 8x8x2-inch pan. Bake at 350 degrees F (175 C) for 30-35 minutes.

Reduced Sugar Brownies
Make Brownies as directed but reduce sugar to ½ cup, add 1½ teaspoons liquid or powdered stevia, and substitute Dutch Processed cocoa or regular cocoa powder. If using liquid stevia, add it to the wet ingredients. If using powdered stevia, combine it with the coconut flour before mixing it into the wet ingredients.

Peanut Butter Brownies

Make Chocolate Nut Brownies as directed but add ½ cup peanut butter and replace the nuts with chopped peanuts.

CREAM CHEESE SQUARES

1 package (8 ounces) cream cheese
⅛ teaspoon salt
⅓ cup honey
½ cup sifted coconut flour
Fruit jam or preserves

Blend together cream cheese, salt, and honey. Add coconut flour and mix thoroughly. Layer batter on the bottom of a greased 11x7x2-inch or 9x9x2-inch pan. Bake at 375 degrees F (190 C) for 18 minutes. Remove from oven and let cool. Spread fruit jam or preserves over the top and cut into bars.

Reduced Sugar Cream Cheese Squares

Make Cream Cheese Squares as directed but replace the honey with gluten-free rice syrup and add ¼ teaspoon stevia.

CHEESE PUFFS

If you like cheese, you will love these airy cracker-like snacks. They taste best hot right out of the oven. Leftovers, if there are any, can be reheated for a minute or so in the oven.

4 egg whites
⅛ teaspoon cream of tartar
⅛ teaspoon salt
⅛ teaspoon onion powder
2 tablespoons coconut flour
2 tablespoons butter, melted
1 cup sharp cheddar cheese, finely shredded

Beat egg whites and cream of tarter until stiff peaks form. Beat in salt and onion powder. In a separate bowl mix coconut flour, butter, and cheese. Fold cheese mixture into egg whites until cheese is evenly distributed. Batter will be a little lumpy. Drop batter in spoon-size mounds 1-inch apart on greased cookie sheet. Bake at 350 degrees F (190 C) for 18-20 minutes or until lightly browned. Serve warm. Makes about 18 crackers.

CHEESE CRACKERS

This is a delicious wheat-free, sugar-free snack that is quick and easy to make. They look like cookies with a crispy cookie-like texture but the taste is distinctly that of a cracker.

½ cup almond flour*
2 eggs
¼ cup butter, melted
¼ teaspoon salt
3 cups sharp cheddar cheese, shredded
½ cup sifted coconut flour

Blend together almond flour, eggs, butter, salt, and cheese. Add coconut flour and kneed the dough in your hands for 2 to 3 minutes. Form dough into 1-inch balls, place on an ungreased cookie sheet, and flatten to a diameter of about 2 to 2½ inches. Bake at 400 degrees F (205 C) for 15 minutes. Makes 16 crackers.

These crackers taste best straight from the oven and slightly crisp. Leftover crackers can be reheated at 400 degrees F (205 C) for about 4 minutes.

*Almond flour can be replaced with nut meal if desired. To make nut meal grind raw nuts in a food processor. You may use almonds, pecans, walnuts, or any nut of your choice.

Onion Cheese Crackers

Make Cheese Crackers as directed and add 1 teaspoon onion power to dough.

Garlic Cheese Crackers

Make Cheese Crackers as directed and add 1 teaspoon garlic power to dough.

5

Cakes

Cakes made with coconut flour taste so good you can't tell them from those made with wheat flour. Using 100 percent coconut flour produces cakes that are light and delicious. Once you taste these cakes, you'll never miss wheat flour cakes again.

In this chapter cake recipes are given first, followed by recipes for cupcakes. Of course, most of the cake recipes can be used to make cupcakes. Some cake recipes include the frosting recipe when the frosting is a characteristic part of the cake. Most frosting recipes, however, are found at the end of the chapter. Use the frosting that most appeals to you for each cake.

All recipes include both regular and reduced sugar versions. You may adjust the sugar content slightly to suit your particular taste. If you want a sweeter cake, you may add a few more tablespoons of sugar; for a less sweet cake, leave a few tablespoons out. Do not remove more than about ¼ cup of sugar as this will change the consistency of the batter. You may also adjust the sugar content of the reduced sugar recipes to make them sweeter if you desire. The reduced sugar recipes have stevia added to help maintain sweetness but they are noticeably less sweet than the regular versions.

I highly recommend that you grease the pans using Dr. Fife's Non-Stick Cooking Oil (page 37). If you do, you won't have any difficulty removing the cakes from the pans, even if they are accidentally over baked. If you don't use this oil, you will need to grease and lightly flour the pans. Grease the pan with butter and lightly flour using coconut flour, cornstarch, or potato flour.

Have all ingredients at room temperature before mixing. In most cases butter and coconut oil should be melted, but not hot. Use butter wherever called for. Do not substitute coconut oil or any other type of oil for butter unless indicated in the recipe. Other oils will work, but butter gives the best flavor and produces the best results.

Coconut milk is used in many of the recipes. If you prefer, you may use whole milk in place of the coconut milk.

Coconut flour should be sifted before combining with other ingredients to break up any lumps in the flour and give an even textured final product.

These cakes, like most baked goods, taste best when served fresh and slightly warm. They even taste good hot right out of the oven. If you store a cake overnight, cover it loosely with plastic wrap and allow for a little air to circulate to prevent the cake from becoming soggy. You may also cover with a cloth dishtowel, which will allow the cake to breathe.

CAKES

YELLOW CAKE

This is a basic cake recipe that can be used to make other types of cakes.

½ cup butter, melted
½ cup coconut milk
12 eggs
1 cup sugar
1 teaspoon salt
1 teaspoon vanilla
1 cup sifted coconut flour
1 teaspoon baking powder
Frosting

Blend together butter, coconut milk, eggs, sugar, salt, and vanilla. Combine coconut flour with baking powder and whisk into batter until there are no lumps. Pour batter into a greased 11x7x2-inch or 9x9x2-inch pan. Bake at 350 degrees F (175 C) for 35-40 minutes or until knife inserted into center comes out clean. Cool. Cover with the frosting of your choice.

Reduced Sugar Yellow Cake

Make Yellow Cake as directed but reduce sugar to ⅓ to ½ cup depending on desired sweetness, add 3 teaspoons powdered or liquid stevia, and increase coconut milk to ¾ cup plus 2 tablespoons. If using liquid stevia, add it to the wet ingredients. If using powdered stevia, combine it with the coconut flour before mixing it into the wet ingredients. Bake at 350 degrees F (175 C) for 40-45 minutes or until knife inserted into center comes out clean. Cool and frost with Low-Sugar Yogurt Frosting or Low-Sugar Meringue Frosting.

Double-Layer Yellow Cake

Make batter for Yellow Cake as directed. Pour batter equally into 2 greased 8 or 9x½ -inch layer cake pans. Bake for 30-35 minutes or until knife inserted into center comes out clean. Cool and remove from baking pan. Fill and frost with frosting of your choice.

Triple-Layer Yellow Cake

¾ cup butter, melted
¾ cup coconut milk
18 eggs
2 ½ cups sugar
1 ½ teaspoons salt
1 ½ teaspoons vanilla
1 ½ cups sifted coconut flour
1 ½ teaspoons baking powder
Frosting

Make cake as directed but bake batter in three 8 or 9x1½ –inch layer cake pans. Fill and frost with frosting of your choice.

MAPLE PECAN CAKE

½ cup butter, melted
½ cup coconut milk
12 eggs
1 cup brown sugar or sucanat
1 teaspoon salt
1 teaspoon maple flavoring
1 cup sifted coconut flour
1 teaspoon baking powder

¾ cup pecans, finely chopped
Frosting

Blend together butter, coconut milk, eggs, sugar, salt, and maple flavoring. Combine coconut flour with baking powder and whisk into batter until there are no lumps. Pour batter into a greased 11x7x2-inch or 9x9x2-inch pan. Fold nuts into batter. Bake at 350 degrees F (175 C) for 35-40 minutes or until knife inserted into center comes out clean. Cool. Cover with Maple Frosting.

Reduced Sugar Maple Pecan Cake
Make Maple Pecan Cake as directed but reduce sugar to ⅓ to ½ cup depending on desired sweetness, add 3 teaspoons powdered or liquid stevia, and increase coconut milk to ¾ cup plus 2 tablespoons. If using liquid stevia, add it to the wet ingredients. If using powdered stevia, combine it with the coconut flour before mixing it into the wet ingredients. Bake at 350 degrees F (175 C) for 40-45 minutes or until knife inserted into center comes out clean. Cool and frost with Low-Sugar Yogurt Frosting or Low-Sugar Meringue Frosting.

CHOCOLATE CHIP CAKE

½ cup butter, melted
½ cup coconut milk
12 eggs
1 cup sugar
1 teaspoon salt
1 teaspoon vanilla
1 cup sifted coconut flour
1 teaspoon baking powder
1 cup sweet chocolate chips
Frosting

Blend together butter, coconut milk, eggs, sugar, salt, and vanilla. Combine coconut flour with baking powder and whisk into batter until there are no lumps. Fold ½ cup chocolate chips into batter. Pour batter into a greased 11x7x2-inch or 9x9x2-inch pan. Sprinkle the remaining chocolate chips evenly over the top of the batter; they will sink into the cake while cooking. Bake at 350 degrees F (175 C) for 35-40 minutes or until knife inserted into center comes out clean. Cool and cover with the frosting of your choice.

Reduced Sugar Chocolate Chip Cake

Make Chocolate Chip Cake as directed but reduce sugar to ⅓ to ½ cup depending on desired sweetness, add 3 teaspoons powdered or liquid stevia, and increase coconut milk to ¾ cup plus 2 tablespoons. If using liquid stevia, add it to the wet ingredients. If using powdered stevia, combine it with the coconut flour before mixing it into the wet ingredients. Bake at 350 degrees F (175 C) for 40-45 minutes or until knife inserted into center comes out clean. Cool and frost with Low-Sugar Yogurt Frosting or Low-Sugar Meringue Frosting.

Butterscotch Cake

Make Chocolate Chip Cake as directed but substitute butterscotch chips for the chocolate chips.

CHOCOLATE CAKE

¾ cup butter or coconut oil
1 cup cocoa powder
12 eggs
½ cup coconut milk or whole milk
1½ cups sugar
1 teaspoon salt
1 teaspoon vanilla
1 cup sifted coconut flour
1 teaspoon baking powder
Marshmallow Frosting

Melt butter in a saucepan over medium heat. Mix in cocoa powder. Remove from heat and set aside. In a bowl mix together eggs, coconut milk, sugar, salt, and vanilla. Stir in cocoa mixture. Combine coconut flour with baking powder and whisk into batter until there are no lumps. Pour batter into a greased 11x7x2-inch or 9x9x2-inch pan. Bake at 350 degrees F (175 C) for 35-40 minutes or until knife inserted into center comes out clean. Cool. Fill layers and cover top and sides of cake with Marshmallow Frosting or the frosting of your choice.

Reduced Sugar Chocolate Cake

Make Chocolate Cake as directed but reduce sugar to 1 cup, add 3 teaspoons liquid or powdered stevia, and substitute Dutch Processed cocoa or regular cocoa powder. If using liquid stevia, add it to the wet ingredients. If using powdered stevia, combine it with the coconut flour before mixing it into the wet ingredients. Bake at 350 degrees F (175 C) for 30-35 minutes or until knife inserted into center comes out clean. Frost with Low-Sugar Yogurt Frosting or Low-Sugar Meringue Frosting.

Double-Layer Chocolate Cake

Make Chocolate Cake as directed. Pour batter equally into 2 greased 8 or 9x½ -inch layer cake pans. Bake for 30-35 minutes or until knife inserted into center comes out clean. Cool and remove from baking pan. Fill and frost with frosting of your choice.

Triple-Layer Chocolate Cake

1 cup butter or coconut oil
1½ cups cocoa powder
18 eggs
¾ cup coconut milk
2¼ cups sugar
1½ teaspoons salt
1½ teaspoons vanilla
1½ cups sifted coconut flour
1½ teaspoons baking powder
Frosting

Make cake as directed but bake batter in three 8 or 9x1½ –inch layer cake pans. Fill and frost with frosting of your choice.

Chocolate Mint Cake

Make Chocolate Cake as directed but add 1 teaspoon peppermint extract to batter if making a single- or double-layer cake. Add 1½ teaspoons of peppermint extract if making a triple-layer cake. Frost and fill with Marshmallow Frosting and sprinkle crushed peppermint candy on top.

GERMAN CHOCOLATE CAKE

This recipe makes a double-layer cake.

⅔ cup butter or coconut oil
1 cup Dutch Processed cocoa powder
8 egg whites
¼ teaspoon cream of tartar
2 whole eggs
8 egg yolks
1 cup coconut milk
2 cups sugar
1 teaspoon salt
1 teaspoon vanilla
1 cup sifted coconut flour
Coconut-Pecan Frosting

Melt butter in a saucepan over medium heat. Add cocoa powder and mix together. Remove from heat and let cool. Beat egg whites and cream of tartar together until stiff peaks form; set aside. In a separate bowl mix together 2 whole eggs, 8 egg yolks, coconut milk, sugar, salt, and vanilla. Stir in cocoa mixture. Whisk coconut flour into batter until there are no lumps. Fold batter into egg whites. Pour batter equally into 2 greased round 8 or 9x1½-inch layer cake pans. Bake at 350 degrees F (175 C) for 35 minutes or until knife inserted into center comes out clean. Cool. Fill layers and cover top and sides of cake with Coconut-Pecan Frosting below.

Coconut-Pecan Frosting

1 cup coconut milk
1½ tablespoons cornstarch
1 cup sugar
2 egg yolks
½ cup butter
1 teaspoon vanilla
1⅓ cup flaked coconut
1 cup pecans, chopped

Mix coconut milk, cornstarch, sugar, egg yolks, and butter in a saucepan. Cook over medium heat, stirring constantly, until mixture thickens. Remove from heat and add vanilla, coconut, and pecans. Let cool before frosting cake.

PINEAPPLE UPSIDE-DOWN CAKE

Topping
1 tablespoon butter, softened
⅓ cup brown sugar or sucanat
1 can (8 ounces) sliced pineapple, drained
7 maraschino cherries
6 pecan halves

Coat bottom and sides of an 8 or 9x1½-inch round layer pan with softened butter. Sprinkle brown sugar over butter. Place 1 pineapple slice in the center of the pan. Cut remaining 3 slices into halves and arrange them around the pineapple in the center of the pan. Put 1 cherry in the center of each pineapple slice. Place pecans around the center pineapple slice. Pour batter (below) over fruit.

Batter
¼ cup butter, melted
6 eggs
½ cup sugar

½ teaspoon salt
½ teaspoon vanilla
½ cup sifted coconut flour
½ teaspoon baking powder

Blend together butter, eggs, sugar, salt, and vanilla. Combine coconut flour with baking powder and whisk into batter until there are no lumps. Pour batter over fruit in pan. Bake at 350 degrees F (175 C) for 30-35 minutes or until knife inserted into center comes out clean. Flip cake over onto heatproof plate. Let pan remain a minute or two. Remove pan. Serve warm.

Reduced Sugar Pineapple Upside-Down Cake

Reduce brown sugar in topping to 3 tablespoons. Reduce sugar in batter to ¼ cup and add 1 teaspoon liquid or powdered stevia. If using liquid stevia, add it to the egg mixture. If using powdered stevia, combine it with the coconut flour before mixing it into the wet ingredients.

WILLIAMSBURG ORANGE CAKE

½ cup butter, melted
12 eggs
¾ cup sugar
1 teaspoon salt
1 teaspoon vanilla
1 cup sifted coconut flour
1 teaspoon baking powder
½ cup golden raisins, cut up
½ cup nuts, finely chopped
1 tablespoon grated orange peel
Williamsburg Butter Frosting

Blend together butter, eggs, sugar, salt, and vanilla. Combine coconut flour with baking powder and whisk into batter until there are no lumps. Fold in raisins, nuts, and orange peel. Pour batter equally into 2 greased

8 or 9x1½ -inch layer cake pans or one 9x9x2-inch pan. Bake at 350 degrees F (175 C) for 30-35 minutes or until knife inserted into center comes out clean. Cool. Cover with Williamsburg Butter Frosting (below).

Williamsburg Butter Frosting

½ cup butter, softened
4½ cups powdered sugar
4 to 5 tablespoons orange flavored liqueur or orange juice
1 tablespoon grated orange peel
Combine all ingredients and beat with an electric beater until smooth.

Reduced Sugar Williamsburg Butter Cake

Make Williamsburg Butter Cake as directed but reduce sugar to ¼ to ⅓ cup depending on desired sweetness, add 3 teaspoons powdered or liquid stevia, and ⅓ cup coconut milk. If using liquid stevia, add it to the wet ingredients. If using powdered stevia, combine it with the coconut flour before mixing it into the wet ingredients. Bake at 350 degrees F (175 C) for 40-45 minutes or until knife inserted into center comes out clean. Cool and frost with Williamsburg Butter Frosting, Low-Sugar Yogurt Frosting, or Low-Sugar Meringue Frosting.

CARROT CAKE

½ cup butter, melted
½ cup coconut milk
12 eggs
1 teaspoon vanilla
1 cup sugar
1 teaspoon salt
1½ teaspoons ground cinnamon
1 teaspoon ground nutmeg
½ teaspoon ground cloves
1 cup sifted coconut flour
1 teaspoon baking powder

2 cups finely grated carrot
½ cup nuts, chopped
Frosting

Combine butter, coconut milk, eggs, and vanilla. In a separate bowl mix together sugar, salt, and spices; stir into wet mixture. Combine coconut flour with baking powder and whisk into batter until there are no lumps. Fold in carrots and nuts. Pour batter equally into 2 greased 8 or 9x1½-inch layer cake pans or one 9x9x2-inch pan. Bake at 350 degrees F (175 C) for 35-40 minutes or until knife inserted into center comes out clean. Cool. Cover with Lemon Swirl Frosting or Lemon Butter Frosting.

Reduced Sugar Carrot Cake

Make Carrot Cake as directed but reduce sugar to ⅓ to ½ cup depending on desired sweetness, add 3 teaspoons powdered or liquid stevia, and increase coconut milk to ¾ cup plus 2 tablespoons. If using liquid stevia, add it to the wet ingredients. If using powdered stevia, combine it with the coconut flour before mixing it into the wet ingredients. Bake at 350 degrees F (175 C) for 40-45 minutes or until knife inserted into center comes out clean. Cool and frost with Low-Sugar Yogurt Frosting or Low-Sugar Meringue Frosting.

LEMON CAKE

½ cup butter, melted
½ cup coconut milk
12 eggs
¾ cup sugar
1 teaspoon salt
3 tablespoons lemon extract
1 cup sifted coconut flour
1 teaspoon baking powder
Frosting

Blend together butter, coconut milk, eggs, sugar, salt, and lemon extract. Combine coconut flour with baking powder and whisk into batter until there are no lumps. Pour batter equally into 2 greased 8 or 9x1½ -inch layer cake pans or one 9x9x2-inch pan. Bake at 350 degrees F (175 C) for 30-35 minutes or until knife inserted into center comes out clean. Cool. Cover with Lemon Butter Frosting.

Reduced Sugar Lemon Cake

Make Lemon Cake as directed but reduce sugar to ¼ to ⅓ cup depending on desired sweetness, add 3 teaspoons powdered or liquid stevia, and increase coconut milk to ¾ cup plus 2 tablespoons. If using liquid stevia, add it to the wet ingredients. If using powdered stevia, combine it with the coconut flour before mixing it into the wet ingredients. Bake at 350 degrees F (175 C) for 40-45 minutes or until knife inserted into center comes out clean. Cool and frost with Low-Sugar Yogurt Frosting or Low-Sugar Meringue Frosting.

SPICE CAKE

½ cup butter, melted
½ cup coconut milk
12 eggs
1 teaspoon vanilla
1 cup sugar
1 teaspoon salt
2 teaspoons ground cinnamon
1 teaspoon ground nutmeg
¼ teaspoon ground allspice
¼ teaspoon ground cloves
¼ teaspoon ground ginger
1 cup sifted coconut flour
1 teaspoon baking powder
Frosting

Combine butter, coconut milk, eggs, and vanilla. In a separate bowl mix together sugar, salt, and spices; stir into wet mixture. Combine coconut flour with baking powder and whisk into batter until there are no lumps. Pour batter into greased 11x7x2-inch or 9x9x2-inch pan. Bake at 350 degrees F (175 C) for 35-40 minutes or until knife inserted into center comes out clean. Cool and frost.

Reduced Sugar Spice Cake

Make Spice Cake as directed but reduce sugar to ⅓ to ½ cup depending on desired sweetness, add 3 teaspoons powdered or liquid stevia, and increase coconut milk to ¾ cup plus 2 tablespoons. If using liquid stevia, add it to the wet ingredients. If using powdered stevia, combine it with the coconut flour before mixing it into the wet ingredients. Bake at 350 degrees F (175 C) for 40-45 minutes or until knife inserted into center comes out clean. Cool and frost with Low-Sugar Yogurt Frosting or Low-Sugar Meringue Frosting.

COFFEE CAKE

Topping
2 cups nuts, chopped
½ cup brown sugar or sucanat
1 teaspoon ground cinnamon
¼ cup butter, melted
Mix all ingredients together and set aside while you make batter.

Batter
½ cup butter, melted
9 eggs
½ cup sugar
¼ cup coconut milk
¾ teaspoon salt
¾ teaspoon vanilla
¾ cup sifted coconut flour
¾ teaspoon baking powder

Mix butter, eggs, sugar, coconut milk, salt, and vanilla. Combine coconut flour with baking powder and whisk into batter until there are no lumps. Pour batter into greased 8x8-inch or 11x7x2-inch pan. Sprinkle topping evenly over batter. Bake at 350 degrees F (175 C) for 35 minutes or until knife inserted into center comes out clean.

Reduced Sugar Coffee Cake

Reduce brown sugar in topping to ¼ cup. Reduce sugar in batter to ¼ cup, increase coconut milk to ⅓ cup, and add 2 teaspoons liquid or powdered stevia. If using liquid stevia, add it to the egg mixture. If using powdered stevia, combine it with the coconut flour before mixing it into the wet ingredients.

CHIFFON CAKE

This recipe makes either a Chiffon or Bundt Cake depending on the type of tube pan used.

12 eggs, separated
½ teaspoon cream of tartar
½ cup butter, melted
½ cup coconut milk
1 cup sugar
1 teaspoon salt
1 teaspoon vanilla
1 cup sifted coconut flour
½ teaspoon baking powder
Glaze Frosting

Combine egg whites and cream of tartar in a large bowl; using an electric beater, beat until stiff peaks form; set aside. In a separate bowl, mix together butter, coconut milk, egg yolks, sugar, salt, and vanilla. Combine coconut flour with baking powder and quickly whisk into batter until moistened. Batter will thicken if stirred for too long or allowed to sit for more than a minute or so; before it thickens, pour it gradually over beaten egg whites, folding with rubber spatula until just blended.

Do not over-mix. Pour batter into a greased tube pan. Bake at 325 degrees F (165 C) for 1¼ hours or until knife inserted into cake comes out clean. Turn pan upside down on center funnel of pan to cool. Let cool for at least 30 minutes, remove cake from pan and cover with one of the Glaze Frostings on pages 107 and 108.

Reduced Sugar Chiffon Cake

Make Chiffon Cake as directed but separate only 10 eggs and put 2 whole eggs (yolks and whites) into egg yolk mixture. Reduce sugar to ⅓ to ½ cup depending on desired sweetness, add 3 teaspoons powdered or liquid stevia, and increase coconut milk to ¾ cup plus 2 tablespoons. If using liquid stevia, add it to the wet ingredients. If using powdered stevia, combine it with the coconut flour before mixing it into the wet ingredients.

VANILLA CUPCAKES

3 tablespoons butter, melted
3 eggs
⅓ cup sugar
¼ teaspoon salt
¼ teaspoon vanilla
¼ cup sifted coconut flour
¼ teaspoon baking powder

Blend together butter, eggs, sugar, salt, and vanilla. Combine coconut flour with baking powder and whisk into batter until there are no lumps. Pour batter into greased muffin cups. Bake at 400 degrees F (205 C) for 15 minutes. Top with frosting of your choice. Makes 6 cupcakes.

Reduced Sugar Vanilla Cupcakes

Make Vanilla Cupcakes as directed but reduce sugar to 3 tablespoons, add 30 drops liquid or ¼ teaspoon powdered stevia, and 2 tablespoons coconut milk. If using powdered stevia, combine it with the coconut flour before mixing it into the wet ingredients. Frost with Low-Sugar Yogurt Frosting or Low-Sugar Meringue Frosting.

CHOCOLATE CUPCAKES

3 tablespoons butter or coconut oil
¼ cup cocoa powder
2 tablespoons coconut milk
3 eggs
¾ cup sugar
¼ teaspoon salt
¼ teaspoon vanilla
¼ cup sifted coconut flour
¼ teaspoon baking powder

In a saucepan at low heat, blend together butter and cocoa powder. Remove from heat and let cool. In a bowl, mix together coconut milk, eggs, sugar, salt, and vanilla. Stir in cocoa mixture. Combine coconut flour with baking powder and whisk into batter until there are no lumps. Pour batter into greased muffin cups. Bake at 400 degrees F (205 C) for 16-18 minutes. Top with frosting of your choice. Makes 6 cupcakes.

Reduced Sugar Chocolate Cupcakes
Make Chocolate Cupcakes as directed but reduce sugar to ⅓ cup, add 30 drops liquid or ¼ teaspoon powdered stevia, and increase coconut milk to ¼ cup. If using powdered stevia, combine it with the coconut flour before mixing it into the wet ingredients. Frost with Low-Sugar Yogurt Frosting or Low-Sugar Meringue Frosting.

PEPPERMINT CUPCAKES

3 tablespoons butter, melted
3 eggs
¼ cup sucanat or sugar

¼ teaspoon salt
¼ teaspoon vanilla
¼ teaspoon peppermint extract
¼ cup sifted coconut flour
¼ teaspoon baking powder
2 tablespoons peppermint candy, crushed

Blend together butter, eggs, sugar, salt, vanilla, and peppermint extract. Combine coconut flour with baking powder and whisk into batter until there are no lumps. Fold in crushed peppermint candy. Pour batter into greased muffin cups. Bake at 400 degrees F (205 C) for 15 minutes. Top with frosting of your choice. Makes 6 cupcakes.

Reduced Sugar Peppermint Cupcakes
Make Peppermint Cupcakes as directed but reduce sugar to 3 tablespoons, add 30 drops liquid or ¼ teaspoon powdered stevia, and 2 tablespoons coconut milk. If using powdered stevia, combine it with the coconut flour before mixing it into the wet ingredients. Frost with Low-Sugar Yogurt Frosting or Low-Sugar Meringue Frosting.

STRAWBERRY SHORTCAKE
These delicious little shortcakes are made in muffin cups.

3 tablespoons butter, melted
3 eggs
3 tablespoons honey
¼ teaspoon salt
¼ teaspoon vanilla
¼ cup sifted coconut flour
¼ teaspoon baking powder

Blend together butter, eggs, honey, salt, and vanilla. Combine coconut flour with baking powder and whisk into batter until there are no lumps. Pour batter into greased muffin cups. Bake at 400 degrees F (205 C) for 15 minutes. Serve topped with fresh strawberries and whipped cream. Makes 6 cakes.

FROSTINGS

MARSHMALLOW FROSING
This is a delicious light and fluffy marshmallow-like frosting.

½ cup sugar
¼ cup light corn syrup
2 tablespoons water
2 egg whites
1 teaspoon vanilla

Mix sugar, corn syrup, and water in saucepan. Cover and heat to a rolling boil over medium heat. Uncover and boil rapidly until candy thermometer reads 242 degrees F (110 C) or until a small amount of the mixture dropped into very cold water forms a firm ball that holds it shape. As the mixture is boiling, beat egg whites until stiff peaks form. With electric beater on medium speed, pour hot syrup very slowly in a thin stream into egg whites. Add vanilla. Beat on high speed until stiff peaks form. Fills and frosts a double-layer cake or a 13x9-inch cake.

VANILLA FROSTING
This is an excellent all-purpose frosting that can be used as a filling and topping on most cakes.

3 cups powdered sugar
⅓ cup butter, softened
1½ teaspoons vanilla
2 tablespoons coconut milk

Combine all ingredients and with an electric beater blend together until smooth. Fills and frosts one double-layer cake. Half recipe frosts one 9x9x2-inch cake.

MAPLE FROSTING

3 cups powdered sugar
⅓ cup butter, softened
½ cup maple syrup

Combine all ingredients and with an electric beater blend together until smooth. Fills and frosts one double-layer cake. Half recipe frosts one 9x9x2-inch cake.

COCONUT CREAM FROSTING

3 cups powdered sugar
⅓ cup butter, softened
2 teaspoons coconut extract
2 tablespoons coconut milk
1 cup flaked coconut

Combine all ingredients, except coconut flakes, and with an electric beater blend together until smooth. Fold in coconut. Fills and frosts one double-layer cake. Half recipe frosts one 9x9x2-inch cake.

LEMON BUTTER FROSTING

3 cups powdered sugar
⅓ cup butter, softened
2 tablespoons lemon juice
1 tablespoon grated lemon peel

Combine all ingredients and with an electric beater blend together until smooth. Fills and frosts one double-layer cake. Half recipe frosts one 9x9x2-inch cake.

CHOCOLATE FROSTING

This is a good frosting for both chocolate and yellow cakes.

⅓ cup butter, softened
2 ounces unsweetened chocolate
2 cups powdered sugar
1½ teaspoons vanilla
2 tablespoons coconut milk or whole milk

In a saucepan at medium heat, melt butter and chocolate. Remove from heat and let cool. Stir in powdered sugar. Beat in vanilla and milk. Fills and frosts one double-layer cake. Half recipe frosts one 9x9x2-inch cake.

Chocolate Nut Frosting

Make Chocolate Frosting as directed and stir in ¼ cup chopped walnuts or pecans.

GLAZE FROSTING

⅓ cup butter, melted
2 cups powdered sugar
1½ teaspoon vanilla
2-4 tablespoons hot water

Combine melted butter, sugar, and vanilla; stir in hot water, 1 tablespoon at a time until glaze is desired consistency.

Lemon Glaze Frosting

Make Glaze Frosting as directed and add 1 tablespoon lemon extract or lemon juice.

Chocolate Glaze Frosting

3 tablespoons butter
2 squares (1 ounce each) unsweetened chocolate
1 cup powdered sugar
¾ teaspoon vanilla
2 tablespoons water

Melt butter and chocolate over low heat. Remove from heat and stir in sugar and vanilla. Add water, 1 tablespoon at a time, until glaze is of desired consistency.

LOW-SUGAR YOGURT FROSTING

Most standard frostings are made almost entirely of sugar and fat and can't be converted into low sugar versions. This is a creamy, soft frosting that is so good you won't miss the traditional sugary ones. The different versions of this frosting (below) make it suitable for almost any type of cake.

1 cup plain yogurt
12 drops liquid stevia
2-3 teaspoons sugar

Blend together all ingredients. Adjust sugar to suit your taste. Frost each slice of cake *just before serving*; allowing the frosting to remain on the cake for too long makes the cake soggy. This recipe makes enough to frost a 8x8x2-inch cake.

Low-Sugar Lemon Yogurt Frosting

1 cup plain yogurt
12 drops liquid stevia

2-3 teaspoons sugar
¼ teaspoon lemon extract

Combine ingredients and follow directions above.

Low-Sugar Fruit Yogurt Frosting

1 cup plain yogurt
12 drops liquid stevia
2-3 teaspoons sugar
1 cup fruit
Blend together yogurt, stevia, and sugar to suit your taste. Mix in fruit. If using small fruit such as blueberries, use them whole. Chop or crush large fruits such as peaches or pineapple.

LOW-SUGAR MERINGUE FROSTING
This is a novel low-sugar, low-carb frosting that gives cakes an elegant look.

3 egg whites
⅛ teaspoon cream of tartar
¼ teaspoon vanilla
2 tablespoons sugar

Beat egg white, cream of tartar, and vanilla until soft peaks form. Add sugar and beat until stiff peaks form. Cook cake until it has about 5 minutes left to bake. Remove the cake from the oven and cover hot cake with meringue frosting. Spread meringue all the way to the edges. Return to oven and bake 7-8 minutes longer or until meringue is lightly browned. Makes enough to frost a 9x9x2-inch cake.

Low-Sugar Lemon Meringue Frosting
Make the Low-Sugar Meringue Frosting as directed but replace the vanilla with ½ teaspoon lemon extract. Bake the cake for the full time required in the recipe; remove it from oven and frost; return to oven

and bake for 4 minutes. Do not overcook. Meringue will not be browned. Goes well with the Yellow, Carrot, Lemon, and Spice cakes.

Low-Sugar Peppermint Meringue Frosting

Make the Low-Sugar Meringue Frosting as directed but replace the vanilla with ⅛ teaspoon peppermint extract. Bake the cake for the full time required in the recipe; remove it from oven and frost; return to oven and bake for 4 minutes. Do not overcook. Meringue will not be browned. This makes an excellent frosting for chocolate cake.

6

Pies and Pastry

Coconut flour can be used to make excellent piecrusts as well as toppings for cobblers and crisps. Pastry for piecrusts can be used with both sweet and savory fillings. Recipes for meat pie fillings are given in Chapter 7. Two versions of most sweet filling recipes are provided, one with full sugar and one with reduced sugar.

The taste and texture of coconut flour piecrust is similar to that of wheat flour crusts. Coconut piecrust dough has a nice texture and rolls out much like wheat flour piecrust. Because coconut flour lacks gluten, one slight difference is that it doesn't hold together quit as well as wheat pie dough. So you need to handle the coconut flour dough a little more carefully to keep it from breaking apart.

The biggest difference between coconut flour and wheat flour piecrusts is the cooking time. Wheat flour crusts require 30-50 minutes. Coconut flour crust generally cooks in only 18-20 minutes at the same temperatures. If you cook it much longer than the prescribed time, the edges tend to burn. This difference in cooking time requires some modifications in the filling used, particularly with fruit fillings. In wheat piecrusts fresh fruit is usually placed into the pie and baked with the crust. The length of time required to cook the crust is sufficient to cook and thicken the filling as well. With coconut flour piecrust you must cook the filling first before putting it into the pie. Cooking is necessary to soften the fruit and thicken the mixture. Of course, if you use a canned filling, this precooking step is already done for you, and no additional cooking is usually necessary.

Five pastry recipes are provided. The first is the Coconut Piecrust recipe that can be used for any type of pie. The second is Coconut Almond Piecrust. This pastry can be used for both sweet and savory pies. It is the best choice for most non-sweet pies such a meat pies. For variety I have included three additional piecrusts: Chopped Nut Piecrust, Peanut Butter Piecrust, and Cream Cheese Piecrust. All are delicious! The Coconut Peanut Butter piecrust goes well with fruit and cream pies. The Coconut Almond piecrust tastes great with any type of pie but gives fruit pies a nice almond flavor—and who doesn't like almonds? If you like cream cheese, you will love the Coconut Cream Cheese piecrust; it's delicious with fruit and cream pies and even meat pies. The piecrust flavors, although mild, give an added dimension to ordinary pies.

PASTRY

If you have made piecrust the traditional way with wheat flour, you know it takes a little practice to produce a good tasting crust. At times it can be frustrating. If the ingredients aren't in the exact proportion or at the right temperature, the results can be disappointing. Making piecrust using coconut flour is much easier. You don't have to be an experienced pie maker or gourmet chef to make a successful piecrust. It's as easy as mixing the ingredients and rolling them out. If you can do that, you can make great tasting coconut flour piecrusts. If the dough is a little dry or a little wet or your kitchen temperate is hot or cold, you will still get good results each time. The hardest part is placing the dough in the pie pan without breaking. Fortunately, pie dough is easily repaired by simply pushing the broken edges back together or by adding a little scrap of dough.

The recipes below make one 9-inch pastry shell for either a single- or a double-crust. The instructions for making the pie shell follow the ingredients for the various crusts.

COCONUT PIECRUST

This tasty all-coconut piecrust is perfect for the coconut lover. It can be used for both single- and double-crust pies of all types. This crust tastes just as good, if not better than traditional wheat pastry. Although easy to mix, the dough needs to be handled carefully because it breaks easily.

Single-Crust

½ cup sifted coconut flour
½ cup flaked coconut
2 eggs
½ tablespoon honey (optional)
¼ cup butter, melted
¼ teaspoon salt

Double-Crust
¾ *cup sifted coconut flour*
¾ *cup flaked coconut*
3 eggs
1 tablespoon honey (optional)
⅓ *cup butter, melted*
¼ *teaspoon salt*

COCONUT ALMOND PIECRUST
This is a delicious all-purpose piecrust. It even tastes better than traditional wheat flour crusts. It browns nicely and cooks evenly. It can be used to make any type of pie, either sweet or savory. It works well for either single-crust or double-crust pies. The dough, however, needs to be handled carefully to avoid breakage, but it is easy to repair.

Single-Crust
½ *cup sifted coconut flour*
½ *cup almond flour/meal**
2 eggs
½ *tablespoon honey (optional)*
¼ *cup butter, melted*
¼ *teaspoon salt*

Double-Crust
¾ *cup sifted coconut flour*
¾ *cup almond flour/meal**
3 eggs
1 tablespoon honey (optional)
5 tablespoons butter, melted
¼ *teaspoon salt*

*If you don't have almond flour available, you can make your own using raw almonds. Chop them into a meal using a food processor.

CHOPPED NUT PIECRUST

Almost any type of nut can be used to make piecrust. Pecans, walnuts, and cashews in combination with coconut flour all give good results. Nuts should be finely chopped or ground. A food processor does an excellent job for this step. Use raw nuts, not roasted. Follow the directions for making Coconut Almond Piecrust, substituting finely chopped nuts for the almond flour.

PEANUT BUTTER PIECRUST

If you like peanuts, you will love this piecrust. The crust has a distinct, yet mild, peanut butter taste. I prefer chunky style peanut butter, but you may use smooth if you like. It is best for single-crust fruit and cream pies. It also makes an excellent crust for chocolate fillings. The dough is very pliable and easy to work with. It holds together well and can be placed and molded into the pie pan without falling apart. Stores well. A single-crust shell can be frozen ahead of time for use later. Store in an airtight freezer-safe plastic bag.

Single-Crust

½ cup sifted coconut flour
¼ cup natural peanut butter
1 egg
2 tablespoons honey
⅛ teaspoon salt
1 tablespoon coconut oil

CREAM CHEESE PIECRUST

The cream cheese gives this crust a distinct flavorful taste. Excellent with fruit fillings.

Single-Crust

½ cup sifted coconut flour
⅔ cup cream cheese

⅛ teaspoon salt
2 tablespoons honey

Double-Crust
¾ cups sifted coconut flour
1 cup plus 2 tablespoons cream cheese
¼ teaspoon salt
3 tablespoons honey

MAKING THE PIE SHELL

Follow the same procedure to make each of the piecrusts above. Sift the coconut flour and set it aside. Thoroughly mix all the remaining ingredients together. Add coconut flour in last and mix it in well to form the dough. Kneed dough with your hands for about 1 minute.

The pie dough is rolled out between two sheets of waxed paper. This keeps your working surface relatively clean, as well as your rolling pin, prevents sticking, and allows you to move the dough with minimal breakage.

Put a sheet of waxed paper on a flat surface. Tape edges of paper down so it doesn't move. Form pastry into a ball; place it on the waxed paper; flatten it with your hand until it is about 6 inches in diameter. Place another sheet of waxed paper on top of the dough. Using a rolling pin flatten the pastry between the two sheets of waxed paper until it is no more than ⅛-inch thick.

The easiest part is over. Getting the dough into the pie pan is the hardest part of the pie making process. Slip a thin, stiff flat object such as a pizza paddle, cookie sheet, or piece of cardboard, underneath the bottom layer of waxed paper. This object will serve as your support for the dough as you lift it and turn it over into the pie pan. Remove the top sheet of waxed paper. Place one hand underneath your support. Place your other hand on top of the dough to hold it in place. Gently, but quickly, flip the dough over and on top of your pie pan. Shape the dough into the pan and remove the remaining sheet of waxed paper. Seal cracks or holes by pressing the edges together; use scraps of pastry to fill in breaks if necessary. Trim overhanging edge of pastry and flute as desired. Fill and bake as directed in each recipe.

116

The edges of the pies will cook much faster than the rest of the crust. To prevent burning on a single-crust shell, coat the top edges of the crust with filling especially if the filling does not completely fill the shell. This thin layer of filling adds moisture to the edge, allowing for evaporation so the crust does not burn. You can also prevent burning by covering the edges with foil. This second method works for both single- and double-crust shells.

Baked Single-Crust Pie Shell

Prick bottom and side several times with a fork to allow steam to escape and avoid distortion of shell during baking. Bake at 400 degrees F (205 C) for 12-15 minutes.

Double-Crust Pie

Leave a little trim of top pastry beyond edge of plate. Fold and roll rim of top pastry under edge of bottom pastry, then press together to seal. Edge can be fluted in any manner you wish for an attractive finish. Cut several slits in the top crust to allow steam to escape. Bake as directed in recipe.

Tart Pastry Shells

Tarts are basically miniature pies. Each pie is an individual serving. Tarts can be double- or single-crust or have only a top crust. Prepare pastry as you would for a full-size pie. The full-size, double-crust recipe makes 4 double-crust tarts, 6 single-crust tarts, or 12 tart tops. The single-crust recipe makes 2 double-crust tarts, 3 single-crust tarts, or 6 tart tops.

Roll out the dough in a thin layer between waxed paper as described above. Nut and cream cheese dough breaks easily. So putting the bottom crust into a tart pan can be tricky. I find it easiest to cut a circle in the flattened dough and place that piece in the bottom of the tart pan. Add strips of dough to the sides of the pan and mold the pieces together, using dough scraps if necessary, to form an even crust.

The top crust is easy. Roll out the dough as before and place it on top of filled tart. Cut or tear off excess and seal the edges. Bake as directed in recipe. You can use tart shells to make any of the pie recipes that follow.

TOPPINGS

MERINGUE

3 egg whites
½ teaspoon vanilla
¼ teaspoon cream of tartar
¼ cup sugar

Beat egg whites, vanilla, and cream of tartar until soft peaks form. Gradually add sugar, beating until stiff and sugar is dissolved. Spread meringue over hot pie filling, spreading all the way to the edge of the pastry (this helps prevent the meringue from shrinking and the edge of crust from burning). Bake at 350 degrees F (175 C) for 12 to 15 minutes, or until meringue is a deep golden brown.

Reduced Sugar Meringue

Make meringue as directed but reduce sugar to 2 tablespoons and add a dash of powdered stevia extract. Be careful not to use too much stevia. A little can go a long way and too much will give the meringue a bitter aftertaste. Use just a tiny bit and gradually add more if you want the meringue to be sweeter.

NUT CRUMB TOPPING

This makes an excellent topping for apple pie. Goes well with any fruit pie. The best nuts to use are coconut, almonds, pecans, and walnuts, but other types of nuts work well too. Finely shredded or flaked coconut can be purchased ready to use without any additional cutting. Other nuts need to be chopped into a coarse meal. The easiest way to chop

Apple pie with Nut Crumb Topping.

nuts is in a food processor. If you do not have a food processor, chop them into a coarse meal by hand.

½ cup finely chopped nuts
¼ cup sucanat or brown sugar
2 tablespoons butter, melted

Mix all ingredients together and sprinkle on top of pie filling. Cook pie as directed.

PIES AND FILLINGS

APPLE PIE

4 tart apples, pared, cored, and thinly sliced
¼ cup raisins (optional)
¾ cup sucanat or sugar
1 teaspoon cinnamon
⅛ teaspoon nutmeg
Dash of salt
2 tablespoons cornstarch or arrowroot flour
¼ teaspoon almond extract
1 unbaked double-crust pie shell

In a large saucepan at medium heat, cook apples in ½ cup water, with lid on, stirring occasionally, until slightly softened (about 10 minutes). Add raisins, sugar, cinnamon, nutmeg, and salt. Mix cornstarch with ¼ cup of water and stir into mixture. Continue to cook until mixture thickens and apples are tender. Remove from heat and stir in almond extract. Fill piecrust with mixture. Add top crust and seal along the edge. Cut several slits in top crust to allow steam to escape. Sprinkle top with sugar. Bake at 400 degrees F (205 C) for 18 minutes.

Reduced Sugar Apple Pie
Make Apple Pie filling as directed but reduce sugar to ¼ cup and add ¼ teaspoon liquid stevia.

Apple Crumb Pie
Make Apple Pie as directed and replace top crust with Nut Crumb Topping.

PEACH PIE

½ cup sucanat or sugar
2 tablespoons butter

2 tablespoons cornstarch or arrowroot flour
½ teaspoon ground cinnamon
⅛ teaspoon ground nutmeg
½ cup water or peach syrup*
4 cups peaches, sliced
¼ teaspoon almond extract
1 unbaked double-crust pie shell

Combine sugar, butter, cornstarch, cinnamon, and nutmeg with water or peach syrup. Cook over medium heat, stirring frequently, until mixture bubbles and thickens. Stir in peaches and cook 4 minutes longer. Mixture should be thick; if not, stir in a little more cornstarch and cook until thickened. Remove from heat and stir in almond extract. Fill piecrust with mixture. Add top crust and seal along the edge. Cut several slits in top crust to allow steam to escape. Sprinkle top with sugar. Bake at 400 degrees F (205 C) for 25-30 minutes.

*Use ½ cup water for fresh peaches and 1 cup water or peach syrup if canned.

Reduced Sugar Peach Pie
Make Peach Pie as directed but omit the sugar and add ¼ teaspoon liquid stevia.

Peach Pie with Nut Crumb Topping
Make Peach Pie as directed but omit the top crust and add Nut Crumb Topping.

CHERRY PIE

¾-1 cup sucanat or sugar
¼ cup cornstarch
¾ cup water or cherry juice
3-4 cups tart red cherries
1 tablespoon butter

¼ teaspoon almond extract
1 unbaked single-crust pie shell
Nut Crumb Topping (page 119)

Combine sugar with cornstarch and water. Cook over medium heat, stirring frequently, until mixture bubbles and thickens; continue to cook 1 minute longer. Mixture will be very thick. Add cherries and butter and cook 1-2 minutes. Mixture should be thick; if not stir in a little more cornstarch and cook until thick. Remove from heat, stir in almond extract, and let stand while preparing pie shell. Bake empty shell at 400 degrees F (205 C) for 8-10 minutes. Remove shell from oven and fill. Sprinkle Nut Crumb Topping over the filling. Bake at 400 degrees F (205 C) for 15 minutes.

RASPBERRY PIE

¾-1 cup sugar
¼ cup cornstarch
¾ cup water
3-4 cups fresh or frozen raspberries
1 tablespoon butter
¼ teaspoon almond extract
1 unbaked single-crust pie shell
Nut Crumb Topping (page 119)

Combine sugar with cornstarch and water. Cook over medium heat, stirring frequently, until mixture bubbles and thickens; continue to cook 1 minute longer. Mixture will be very thick. Add raspberries and butter and cook 1-2 minutes. Remove from heat, stir in almond extract, and let stand while preparing pie shell. Bake empty shell at 400 degrees F (205 C) for 8-10 minutes. Remove shell from oven and fill. Sprinkle Nut Crumb Topping over the filling. Bake at 400 degrees F (205 C) for 15 minutes.

BLUEBERRY PIE

¾ cup sucanat or sugar
¼ cup cornstarch or arrowroot flour
¾ cup water
4 cups blueberries
¼ teaspoon vanilla extract
1 unbaked single-crust pie shell
Nut Crumb Topping (page 119)

Combine sugar with cornstarch and water. Cook over medium heat, stirring frequently, until mixture bubbles and thickens; continue to cook 1 minute longer. Mixture will be very thick. Add blueberries and butter and cook 1 to 2 minutes. Remove from heat, stir in vanilla, and let stand while preparing pie shell. Bake empty shell at 400 degrees F (205 C) for 8-10 minutes. Remove shell from oven and fill. Sprinkle Nut Crumb Topping over the filling. Bake at 400 degrees F (205 C) for 15 minutes.

STRAWBERRY GLACE PIE

6 cups strawberries, sliced
1 cup sugar
3 tablespoons cornstarch or arrowroot flour
½ cup water
3 ounces cream cheese, softened
1 baked single-crust pie shell

Mash enough strawberries to make 1 cup. Mix with sugar, cornstarch, and water and cook over medium heat, stirring constantly, until mixture boils and thickens. Continue to cook for 1 minute. Remove from heat and set aside. Beat cream cheese until smooth. Spread on the bottom of cooled baked pie shell. Fill shell with remaining strawberries, and pour cooked strawberry mixture on top. Refrigerate about 3 hours or until set. Serve chilled.

Reduced Sugar Strawberry Glace Pie

Omit the sugar and cornstarch. Combine mashed strawberries, 1 teaspoon liquid stevia, 1 envelope (1 tablespoon) unflavored gelatin, and ½ cup of boiling water. Stir and let sit for 5 minutes for gelatin to dissolve. Layer cream cheese on the bottom of a baked pie shell; ¼ cup sugar may be mixed with the cream cheese to increase sweetness if desired. Fill shell with sliced strawberries and pour mashed strawberry mixture on top. Refrigerate about 3 hours or until set.

PUMPKIN PIE

1 can (15 to 16 ounces) pumpkin
¾ cup sucanat or sugar
¾ teaspoon salt
1 teaspoon ground cinnamon
½ teaspoon ground ginger
¼ teaspoon ground nutmeg
¼ teaspoon ground cloves
4 slightly beaten eggs
1 unbaked single-crust pie shell

Mix together all ingredients and pour into pastry shell. Coat the entire inside crust, including the top edge, with a thin layer of filling to prevent burning. Bake at 400 degrees F (205 C) for 35-40 minutes or until knife inserted in center comes out clean. Cool. Just before serving top with whipped cream.

Reduced Sugar Pumpkin Pie

Make Pumpkin Pie as directed but reduce sugar to ½ cup and add ¼ teaspoon stevia.

FROZEN COCONUT PIE

¾ cup coconut milk
1 ¼ cup flaked coconut

¾ *cup sugar*
½ *teaspoon almond extract*
1½ *cups whipped cream, whipped*
1 *baked single-crust pie shell*

Combine coconut milk, coconut, sugar, and almond extract. Let mixture sit for about 5 minutes to allow sugar to dissolve. Fold in whipped cream. Pour into baked pastry shell and freeze for at least 4 hours. Thaw for 10-15 minutes before cutting pie into slices.

Reduced Sugar Frozen Coconut Pie
Make Frozen Coconut Pie as directed but reduce sugar to ¼ cup and add ¼ teaspoon liquid stevia.

VANILLA CREAM PIE

¾ *cup sugar*
¼ *teaspoon salt*
2½ *cups coconut milk*
¼ *cup cornstarch*
4 *slightly beaten egg yolks*
2 *tablespoons butter*
½ *tablespoon vanilla*
1 *baked single-crust pie shell*

In a saucepan, combine sugar, salt, and 2 cups of coconut milk. Cook over medium heat until mixture begins to boil; reduce heat. Combine the remaining ½ cup of coconut milk with cornstarch and stir into hot mixture, stirring constantly until mixture thickens. Cook 1 minute longer. Remove from heat. Slowly stir at least ½ cup of hot mixture into yolks. Put saucepan back on heat and stir yolk mixture into saucepan; cook 1 minute, stirring constantly. Remove from heat. Add butter and vanilla. Pour into cooled baked pastry shell. To prevent skin from forming on surface of filling as it cools, put waxed paper directly on top of hot filling. Let cool and refrigerate at least 2 hours. Remove waxed paper and top pie with whipped cream.

Reduced Sugar Vanilla Cream Pie

Make pie as directed but reduce sugar to ⅓ cup and add ¼ teaspoon liquid stevia.

Chocolate Cream Pie

Prepare Vanilla Cream Pie, increasing sugar to 1½ cups and cornstarch to ⅓ cup. In a saucepan over medium heat, melt two 1-ounce squares of unsweetened chocolate. Add sugar, salt, coconut milk, and cornstarch and cook as directed.

Banana Cream Pie

Slice 3 bananas and put into cooled baked pastry shell. Pour Vanilla Cream or Chocolate Cream Pie filling over bananas.

Coconut Cream Pie

Add 1 cup of grated or flaked coconut to pie filling to hot mixture before filling pie shell.

Strawberry Cream Pie

Mix 3 cups fresh sliced strawberries into mixture just before filling the pie shell.

LEMON CHIFFON PIE

1 envelope unflavored gelatin
1 cup sugar
½ teaspoon salt
4 egg yolks
⅓ cup lemon juice
⅔ cup water
½ teaspoon grated lemon peel
4 egg whites
½ cup whipping cream, whipped
1 baked single-crust pie shell

In saucepan, combine gelatin, ½ cup of the sugar, and salt. In bowl mix together egg yolks, lemon juice, and water. Stir into gelatin mixture. Cook over medium heat, stirring constantly until mixture comes to a boil and gelatin dissolves. Remove from heat and stir in lemon peel. Chill, stirring occasionally, until partially set but still pourable (about 30-45 minutes). With an electric beater, beat egg whites until soft peaks form. Gradually add remaining sugar, beating until stiff peaks form. Fold in whipped cream and partially set gelatin mixture. Put into cooled, baked pastry shell. Chill until firm, about 3 to 5 hours.

Reduced Sugar Lemon Chiffon Pie

Make Lemon Chiffon Pie as directed but reduce sugar in gelatin mixture and in egg whites to ¼ cup each. Reduce lemon juice to ¼ cup and add ¼ teaspoon liquid stevia to egg yolk mixture.

STRAWBERRY CHIFFON PIE

2 cups fresh strawberries, sliced
¾ cup sugar
⅓ cup water
1 envelope unflavored gelatin
1 tablespoon lemon juice
2 egg whites
½ cup whipping cream, whipped
1 baked single-crust pie shell

Crush strawberries; add ½ cup of the sugar; let stand for 30 minutes. In the meantime, bring water to a boil, remove from heat, and let sit for 1 minute. Stir in gelatin and allow to dissolve for about 5 minutes. Stir the gelatin, water, and lemon juice, with the crushed strawberries. Chill, stirring occasionally, until partially set but still pourable (about 45 minutes). Beat egg whites to soft peaks; gradually add the remaining ¼ cup sugar, beating until stiff peaks form. Fold into chilled strawberry mixture, then fold in whipped cream. Fill cooled baked pastry shell. Chill until firm, about 3 to 5 hours.

Reduced Sugar Strawberry Chiffon Pie

Make pie as directed but omit lemon juice and sugar, increase strawberries to 3 cups, and add 1 teaspoon liquid stevia to crushed strawberries; ¼ cup sugar may be added to increase sweetness if desired.

CHOCOLATE CHIFFON PIE

1 envelope unflavored gelatin
3 egg yolks
¼ teaspoon salt
1 teaspoon vanilla
¾ cup sugar
2 1-ounce squares unsweetened chocolate
3 egg whites
½ cup whipped cream, whipped
1 baked single-crust pie shell

Soften gelatin in ¼ cup cold water. In mixing bowl, beat egg yolks, salt, vanilla, and ½ cup of the sugar and set aside. In a saucepan, combine chocolate and ½ cup water; stir over low heat until melted; add softened gelatin and stir to dissolve. Mix egg yolk mixture into chocolate mixture, stir 1 minute, and remove from heat. Chill, stirring occasionally, until mixture is partially set but still pourable (about 15-30 minutes). With an electric better, beat egg whites to soft peaks. Gradually add ¼ cup sugar, beating to stiff peaks. Combine with whipped cream and fold in chilled chocolate mixture until blended. Fill baked pie shell. Chill until firm.

Reduced Sugar Chocolate Chiffon Pie

Make Chocolate Chiffon Pie as directed but reduce sugar in egg yolk mixture and egg whites to 2 tablespoons each. Add ¼ teaspoon liquid stevia to egg yolk mixture.

BLACK BOTTOM CUSTARD PIE

Bottom Layer
1 can (14 ounces) coconut milk
4 beaten egg yolks
½ cup sugar
2 tablespoons cornstarch
1 teaspoon vanilla
1 6-ounce package (1 cup) semisweet chocolate chips
1 baked single-crust pie shell
Top Layer
1 envelope unflavored gelatin
¼ cup water
½ teaspoon almond extract
4 egg whites
½ cup sugar
Sliced almonds, toasted

Mix coconut milk and egg yolks together, stir in ½ cup sugar and cornstarch. Cook and stir over medium heat until custard thickens. Remove from heat and add vanilla. Put 1 cup of hot custard in a separate bowl along with chocolate chips, stir until melted (you will have some custard left over to be used below). Pour into baked pastry shell and chill.

Meanwhile, soften gelatin by combining it with ¼ cup water and remaining *hot* custard. Stir until dissolved. Mix in almond extract. Chill until slightly thickened. Beat egg whites until soft peaks form; gradually add ½ cup sugar; beat again until stiff peaks form. Fold into chilled custard-gelatin mixture. Remove half filled pie from refrigerator and pour mixture on top of chocolate layer. Sprinkle top with lightly toasted sliced almonds. Chill until set.

LEMON MERINGUE PIE

1½ cups sugar
1½ cups water

⅓ cup plus 1 tablespoon cornstarch
3 egg yolks, slightly beaten
3 tablespoons butter
½ teaspoon grated lemon peel
½ cup lemon juice
1 unbaked single-crust pie shell
Meringue (page 118)

Mix sugar and 1 cup of water in saucepan and heat until it boils. Reduce heat. Mix ½ cup water with cornstarch and stir into hot mixture. Cook over medium heat, stirring constantly, until mixture thickens; cook and stir 1 minute longer. Remove from heat. Gradually stir half of the hot mixture into egg yolks and then stir egg yolks into the rest of the hot mixture in saucepan. Return to heat and cook for 1 minute, stirring constantly. Remove from heat; stir in butter, lemon peel, and lemon juice. Bake empty pie shell at 400 degrees F (205 C) for 8 minutes. Remove shell from oven and pour in hot filling. Spoon meringue on top of hot pie filling; spread over filling, carefully sealing meringue to edge of crust to prevent shrinking. Bake at 400 degrees F (205 C) 10-12 minutes, until deep golden brown. Cool on wire rack and then chill.

Reduced Sugar Lemon Meringue Pie
Make Lemon Meringue Pie as directed but reduce sugar to ½ cup, reduce lemon juice to ¼ cup, reduce cornstarch to ⅓ cup, and add ½ teaspoon liquid stevia.

PINEAPPLE CREAM PIE

¾ cup sucanat or sugar
3 tablespoons cornstarch or arrowroot flour
½ teaspoon salt
1 1-pound 4½-ounce can (2½ cups) crushed pineapple, undrained
1 cup sour cream
1 tablespoon lemon juice
2 slightly beaten egg yolks

1 baked single-crust pie shell
Meringue (118)

In a saucepan, combine sugar, cornstarch, and salt. Stir in undrained pineapple, sour cream, and lemon juice until thoroughly mixed. Cook over medium heat until mixture thickens and bubbles; cook and stir 2 minutes longer. Remove from heat. Slowly stir at least ½ cup of hot mixture into yolks. Put saucepan back on heat and stir yolk mixture into saucepan; cook 1 minute, stirring constantly. Remove from heat. Pour into cooled baked pastry shell. Spoon meringue on top of hot pie filling; spread over filling, carefully sealing meringue to edge of crust to prevent shrinking. Bake at 400 degrees F (205 C) 10-12 minutes, until deep golden brown. Cool on wire rack before serving.

Reduced Sugar Pineapple Cream Pie
Make Pineapple Cream Pie as directed but omit lemon juice, reduce sugar to ¼ cup, and add ¼ teaspoon liquid stevia.

COCONUT PECAN PIE
For added pecan flavor use the Chopped Nut Piecrust made with pecans.

4 beaten eggs
1 cup sucanat or brown sugar
½ cup melted butter
4 teaspoons lemon juice
1 teaspoon vanilla
1 cup grated coconut
1 unbaked single-crust pie shell
⅔ cup pecan halves

Beat eggs, sugar, melted butter, lemon juice, and vanilla together until well blended; stir in coconut. Pour into unbaked pie shell. Filling will not reach the top of the crust. Spread a layer of filling along the top of the crust to prevent over browning. Carefully layer pecan halves on top of pie filling. Bake at 350 degrees F for 40 minutes. Remove from oven and cool on wire rack.

Reduced Sugar Coconut Pecan Pie
Follow directions above but reduce lemon juice to 1 tablespoon, reduce sugar to ⅓ cup, and add ¼ teaspoon liquid stevia.

COBBLERS AND CRISPS

PEACH COBBLER

Peach Filling
2 tablespoons cornstarch or arrowroot flour
¼ teaspoon ground cinnamon
⅛ teaspoon ground nutmeg
1 cup water or peach syrup*
4 cups sliced peaches

Combine cornstarch or arrowroot flour, ground cinnamon, nutmeg, and water in a saucepan. Cook and stir until thickened. Add peaches. Cook until peaches are hot and liquid is thick. Pour into ungreased 2-quart casserole dish.

*If you use fresh peaches, use ½ cup water. If you use canned peaches, use 1 cup of the syrup.

Topping
4 eggs
¼ cup butter or coconut oil, melted
⅓ cup sucanat or sugar
1 teaspoon vanilla
¼ teaspoon salt
½ cup sifted coconut flour
¼ teaspoon baking powder

Blend together eggs, butter, sugar, vanilla, and salt. Combine coconut flour with baking powder and stir into batter until there are no lumps remaining. Batter will be runny. Pour the batter evenly over the top of the fruit. Bake at 400 degrees F (205 C) for 25 to 30 minutes or until top is a dark golden brown. Makes 6 servings.

Reduced Sugar Peach Cobbler
Reduce sugar in topping to 2 tablespoons and add 30 drops of liquid stevia.

Blueberry Cobbler
Omit the cinnamon and nutmeg and substitute 4 cups of blueberries for the peaches.

Cherry Cobbler
Substitute 4 cups of pitted red tart cherries for the peaches. Omit the cinnamon and nutmeg and add ¾ cup sugar and ¼ teaspoon almond extract to cherry filling and increase cornstarch to 3 tablespoons.

Apple Cobbler
Combine 1 cup sugar, 2 tablespoons cornstarch or arrowroot flour, ½ teaspoon ground cinnamon, ¼ teaspoon nutmeg, and 6 cups sliced apples. Cook and stir over medium heat until almost tender (about 7 minutes). Bake as directed.

PEACH CRISP

Filling
4 cups peaches, peeled and sliced
2 tablespoons cornstarch or arrowroot flour
½ teaspoon ground cinnamon
⅛ teaspoon ground nutmeg
¼ cup sucanat or brown sugar

Topping
¾ cup finely chopped nuts
¾ cup sucanat or brown sugar
½ cup sifted coconut flour
¾ cup grated or flaked coconut
½ cup butter or coconut oil, softened
Dash of salt

In a bowl, mix peaches, cornstarch, cinnamon, nutmeg, and sugar together. Arrange peach mixture in a 8x8x2-inch baking dish and set aside. Mix all the topping ingredients together and layer on top of the peaches. Bake at 375 degrees F (190 C) for 35 minutes or until topping is browned. Serve with whipped cream or yogurt.

Reduced Sugar Peach Crisp
Make Peach Crisp as directed but delete the sugar from the peach mixture. Reduce sugar in topping to ¼ cup.

Apple Crisp
Make Peach Crisp as directed but substitute tart apples for the peaches.

Cherry Crisp
Make Peach Crisp as directed but substitute tart red cherries for the peaches and omit the cinnamon and nutmeg. Add ¼ teaspoon of almond extract to filling.

7

Savory Dishes

Coconut flour can be used in making savory main and side dishes as well as breads and desserts. In this chapter you will find a variety of non-bread recipes. Many of the recipes in this chapter like Meat Loaf, Chicken and Dumpling Casserole, and Chicken Pot Pie are familiar to most people. The unique feature of these recipes is the use of coconut flour. Adding coconut four to familiar recipes can greatly increase the fiber content of the foods, making them healthier and less fattening.

MEAT LOAF

½ cup coconut flour
3 eggs
1 cup finely chopped onion
½ cup chopped bell pepper
1 teaspoon salt
½ teaspoon black pepper
⅛ teaspoon thyme
⅛ teaspoon marjoram
1 pound ground beef
1 16-ounce can tomato sauce

Combine coconut flour, eggs, chopped onion, bell pepper, salt, black pepper, thyme, and marjoram in a bowl. Add ground beef and 1 cup (8 ounces) of tomato sauce and mix well. Shape mixture into a loaf and place into a baking dish. Pour the remaining 1 cup of tomato sauce over the top of the loaf. Bake at 350 degrees F (175 C) for 1¼ hours. Makes 6 to 8 servings.

VEGETABLE MEAT LOAF

½ cup coconut flour
4 eggs
1 cup finely chopped onion
1 cup chopped bell pepper
2 cups chopped spinach

½ cup finely chopped celery
1½ teaspoons salt
½ teaspoon lemon pepper
¼ teaspoon onion powder
1 pound ground beef
1 8-ounce can tomato sauce

Combine all ingredients with ½ cup (4 ounces) of tomato sauce and mix well. Shape mixture into a loaf and place into a baking dish. Pour the remaining tomato sauce over the top of the loaf. Bake at 350 degrees F (175 C) for 1¼ hours. Makes 6 to 8 servings.

ITALIAN MEAT LOAF

1 cup finely chopped onion
½ cup finely chopped bell pepper
8-10 cloves garlic, chopped
1 pound ground beef
2 cups cheese, chopped into ½-inch cubes
1 3-ounce can chopped mushrooms (drained)
3 eggs
½ cup coconut flour
1½ teaspoons salt
½ teaspoon pepper
¼ teaspoon thyme
½ teaspoon oregano
1 8-ounce can tomato sauce

Sauté onion, bell pepper, and garlic until tender crisp. Combine cooked vegetables with ground beef, cheese, mushrooms, eggs, coconut flour, salt, pepper, thyme, and oregano in a bowl and mix well. Form mixture into a loaf and place into baking dish. Pour tomato sauce over the top. Bake at 350 degrees F (175 C) for 1¼ hours. Makes 6 to 8 servings.

HIGH FIBER HAMBURGERS

1 pound ground beef
½ cup coconut flour
½ teaspoon salt
¼ teaspoon pepper
½ teaspoon onion powder
2 eggs

Combine all ingredients and mix thoroughly. Shape burgers into 6 patties about ½-inch thick. Broil in oven for 6 minutes, turn and broil 4 minutes or until done. Patty can be eaten separately or on a gluten-free bun.

COCONUT FRIED CHICKEN

⅓ cup coconut flour
1 teaspoon paprika
¼ teaspoon pepper
1 teaspoon salt
1 whole chicken, cut up
Coconut oil for frying

Heat coconut oil ¼-inch deep in skillet until a drop of water sizzles. Combine flour, paprika, pepper, and salt in a paper or plastic bag; add 2 or 3 pieces of chicken at a time and shake. Brown meaty pieces first, then add remaining pieces. Brown one side; turn with tongs. When lightly browned, 15 to 20 minutes, reduce heat; cover tightly. Cook 30 to 40 minutes, or until tender. Uncover last 10 minutes. Makes 4 servings.

Coconut Fried Fish
Use the same coating as the Coconut Fried Chicken but omit the pepper and add ¼ teaspoon lemon pepper. Fish requires less cooking so reduce time as needed.

CHICKEN FRIED STEAK

⅓ *cup coconut flour*
¼ *teaspoon pepper*
½ *teaspoon paprika*
½ *teaspoon onion powder*
1 pound ground beef
1 egg
1 teaspoon salt
Coconut oil for frying

Mix coconut flour, pepper, paprika, and onion powder and set aside. Mix together ground beef, egg, and salt and form into 6 equal-sized patties about ½-inch thick. Coat both sides of patties in flour mixture. Sprinkle remaining flour mixture on top of patties. Heat coconut oil in skillet until a drop of water sizzles. Place meat patties in hot skillet, cover, and cook until bottom coating is lightly browned (about 6-8 minutes). Turn the patties over and brown the other side, uncovered. Makes 6 patties.

HAM POPOVER DELIGHT

This tasty dish consists of coconut flour popovers smothered in ham gravy. Makes an excellent meal for breakfast or hearty side dish or main coarse for dinner.

¼ *cup chopped onion*
1 clove garlic, chopped
2 tablespoons butter
1 tablespoon cornstarch
½ *cup water*
½ *cup ham, diced*
¾ *cup coconut milk*
⅛ *teaspoon ground cloves*
Salt and pepper
6 Popovers (page 49)

Sauté onion and garlic in butter until tender. Stir cornstarch into water and add to vegetables along with ham and coconut milk. Stirring frequently, cook until mixture thickens. Add cloves and salt and pepper to taste. Simmer for 10 minutes stirring as needed. Serve gravy over hot, freshly baked popovers. Makes 6 servings.

TAMALE PIE

Filling

2 tablespoons coconut oil
1 pound ground beef
1 medium onion, chopped
1 green pepper, chopped
2 8-ounce cans tomato sauce
1 12-ounce can black olives
1 teaspoon salt
2 to 3 teaspoons chili powder
Dash of cayenne

Cook oil, meat, onion, and green pepper in a large skillet until meat is lightly browned and vegetables are tender. Stir in tomato sauce, olives, salt, chili powder, and cayenne. Simmer 10 minutes. Pour into 13x9x2-inch baking dish.

Topping

5 cups water
¾ cup yellow cornmeal
1 teaspoon salt
1 teaspoon chili powder
¼ cup butter
¾ cup coconut flour
1 cup whole kernel corn
6 ounces sharp cheddar cheese (1½ cups), shredded

Combine 4 cups of water, cornmeal, salt, chili powder, and butter in saucepan and heat, stirring constantly until mixture is slightly thickened (about 8 minutes). Stir in remaining cup of water, coconut flour, and corn. Continue to cook and stir until thick. Spoon over hot meat mixture. Top with shredded cheese. Bake at 400 degrees F (205 C) for 40 minutes. Makes 8 servings.

SLOPPY JOE

2 tablespoons coconut oil
1 pound ground beef
1 medium-size yellow onion, chopped
½ bell pepper, chopped
¼ cup coconut flour
1 teaspoon salt
⅛ teaspoon pepper
1 cup barbeque sauce
¼ cup water

Heat oil in skillet. Add ground beef, onion, and bell pepper. Cook until beef is browned and vegetables are tender. Stir in coconut flour, salt, pepper and cook an additional 3 to 5 minutes, stirring frequently. Add barbeque sauce and water and mix thoroughly. Remove from heat. Spoon mixture between split gluten-free buns or use as a topping on baked potato. Tastes good served on top of Drop Biscuits (page 46), Cornbread (page 48), or Popovers (page 49). Serves 6.

CHILI WITH BEANS

1 medium-size yellow onion, chopped
1 medium-size bell pepper, chopped
4 cloves garlic, finely chopped
1 pound ground beef
2 tablespoons coconut oil or lard
2 cups water

1 15-ounce can tomatoes, do not drain
2 15-ounce cans red kidney beans, do not drain
¼ cup coconut flour
2 teaspoons chili powder
1 teaspoon paprika
1 teaspoon cumin
1 teaspoon salt
⅛ teaspoon crushed red chili peppers

Sauté onions, peppers, garlic, and beef with oil in a large pot over moderate heat until beef is lightly browned and vegetables are tender. Add remaining ingredients and simmer for 30 minutes, stirring occasionally. Serve with Drop Biscuits (page 46) or Cornbread (page 48). Serves 6.

SPAGHETTI WITH MEATBALLS

Meatballs
½ pound ground beef
¼ cup coconut flour
2 eggs
½ teaspoon salt
⅛ teaspoon pepper
¼ teaspoon onion powder

Combine ingredients and mix well. Form meat mixture into small balls about 1-inch in diameter. Cook as directed below.

Spaghetti Sauce
2 tablespoons extra virgin olive oil
1 medium onion, chopped
½ bell pepper, chopped
8 cloves garlic, minced
4 ounces fresh mushrooms, chopped
1 can (32 ounces) tomato sauce
1 teaspoon salt

½ teaspoon pepper
1 teaspoon oregano
¼ teaspoon thyme
¼ teaspoon marjoram
Gluten-free noodles

At moderate heat, cook meatballs in a skillet with extra virgin olive oil. Add onion, bell pepper, and garlic and cook until meat is browned on all sides and vegetables are tender. Add mushrooms, tomato sauce, salt, pepper, oregano, thyme, and marjoram, cover and simmer for 20 to 30 minutes stirring occasionally. Serve over hot gluten-free rice or corn noodles.

MEATBALLS WITH MUSHROOM SAUCE

Meatballs (page 142)
8 ounces fresh mushrooms, sliced
1 cup onion, finely chopped
1 tablespoon cornstarch or arrowroot flour
1 can (14 ounces) coconut milk
2 tablespoons butter
1 teaspoon salt
¼ teaspoon pepper

Sauté meatballs, mushrooms, and onions in 1 tablespoon of coconut oil until meat is lightly browned on all sides and vegetables are tender. Combine cornstarch with coconut milk and stir into meatball mixture. Add butter, salt, and pepper. Simmer, stirring frequently, for about 15 minutes. Serve over gluten-free rice or corn pasta or hot steamed vegetables.

GERMAN MEATBALLS

Meatballs (page 142)
½ cup onion, finely chopped

2 cups chicken or beef broth, prepared or homemade
3 tablespoons cornstarch or arrowroot flour
1 3-ounce can chopped mushrooms, drained
½ teaspoon dried dill
Salt and pepper
½ cup sour cream

At moderate heat, cook meatballs in a skillet with 2 tablespoons of butter. Add onion and cook until meat is browned on all sides and onion is tender. Stir cornstarch into broth and add to meatballs. Add mushrooms, cover, and simmer about 20 minutes stirring frequently. Remove from heat and add dill and salt and pepper to taste. Stir in sour cream. Serve over gluten-free rice or corn pasta or hot steamed vegetables.

MEATBALLS AND CHEESE SAUCE

Meatballs (page 142)
2 tablespoons coconut oil or butter
8 ounces mushrooms, sliced
½ onion, chopped
1 tablespoon cornstarch or arrowroot flour
1 can (14 ounces) coconut milk
1 ½ cups sharp cheddar cheese, shredded
1 teaspoon salt
¼ teaspoon pepper

At medium heat, cook meatballs in a skillet with 2 tablespoons of coconut oil or butter. Add onion and cook until meat is browned on all sides and onion is tender. Stir cornstarch into coconut milk. Add coconut milk and mushrooms to skillet, cover, and simmer about 10 minutes. Stir in the cheese and continue to cook over low heat until melted. Add salt and pepper. Serve over gluten-free rice or corn pasta or hot steamed vegetables.

SPLIT PEA SOUP

2 ¼ cups green split peas
1 meaty ham bone (1 ½ pounds)
1 ½ cups onion, chopped
10 cloves garlic, chopped
1 cup celery, diced
1 cup carrots, diced
½ cup coconut flour
1 ½ teaspoons salt
½ teaspoon pepper
¼ teaspoon marjoram

Rinse peas. Combine peas with two quarts water and ham bone. Bring to boiling, cover, reduce heat, and simmer 2 hours. Remove bone, cut off meat, and return meat to soup. Add onion, garlic, celery, carrots, coconut flour, salt, pepper, and marjoram. Cover and simmer approximately 2 hours until peas are tender, stirring occasionally. Serves 6 to 8.

PASTA WITH SHRIMP SAUCE

¼ cup coconut flour
2 tablespoons coconut oil
¾ cup onion, diced
1 ¼ cup coconut milk
¾ cup baby shrimp
½ teaspoon chili powder
½ teaspoon fish sauce*
Juice of ½ lemon
1 cup sharp cheddar cheese, shredded

Heat coconut oil and flour in a saucepan until flour is lightly browned. Add onion and cook until tender (about 5 minutes), stirring occasionally. Add coconut milk, shrimp, chili powder, fish sauce, and lemon. Simmer for 15 minutes. Add cheese and continue to cook until melted. Pour hot

Shrimp Sauce over cooked gluten-free rice or corn pasta and serve. Makes 3 servings.

*Fish sauce is available in the Asian food section of your grocery store. It is also sold in health food stores and Asian markets.

Vegetables with Shrimp Sauce
Follow the directions for making the Pasta with Shrimp Sauce. Omit the pasta and pour the Shrimp Sauce over hot cooked vegetables. Goes well with any of the following: broccoli, cauliflower, asparagus, zucchini, green beans, Brussels sprouts, or potatoes.

Biscuits and Shrimp Sauce
Follow the directions for making the Pasta with Shrimp Sauce. In place of the pasta pour the Shrimp Sauce over hot biscuits.

Eggs and Shrimp Sauce
Follow the directions for making the Pasta with Shrimp Sauce. In place of the pasta pour the Shrimp Sauce over poached or hard boiled eggs.

CHICKEN AND DUMPLING CASSEROLE
This recipe is good for using leftover chicken. The chicken bones can be stewed for several hours in a little water to make the broth.

Stew
2 cups chicken broth
1 cup onion, chopped
1 stalk celery, chopped
2 red potatoes, chopped*
½ cup peas
1 cup cut-up chicken
2 tablespoons cornstarch or arrowroot flour
½ cup coconut milk
½ teaspoon salt

¼ *teaspoon pepper*
½ *teaspoon marjoram*

In a large saucepan, bring broth to a boil. Add onion, celery, potato, peas, and chicken. Reduce heat and simmer for 30 minutes. Mix cornstarch into coconut milk and stir into stew. Add salt, pepper, and marjoram and simmer, stirring occasionally, for 5 to 10 minutes. Taste and add more salt if needed. While stew is cooking, make the dumpling batter.

*You may substitute 1-2 cups of chopped cauliflower for the potato.

Dumplings

4 eggs
¼ *cup butter or coconut oil, melted*
¼ *teaspoon salt*
⅓ *cup sifted coconut flour*
¼ *teaspoon baking powder*

Blend together eggs, butter, and salt. Combine coconut flour with baking powder and whisk into batter until there are no lumps.

Pour hot stew into a 2-quart casserole dish. Drop batter by the spoonful on top of stew, making 4 large dumplings. Bake at 400 degrees F (205 C) for 15 to 20 minutes. Serves 4.

Cheese Dumplings

Make Dumplings as directed and add 1 cup shredded sharp cheddar cheese.

Herb Dumplings

Make Dumplings as directed and add ½ teaspoon of dried herbs. Good herbs to use are sage, thyme, marjoram, and rosemary.

Indian-Style Dumplings
Make Dumplings as directed and add ½ teaspoon of curry powder or garam masala.

HAMBURGER PIE

1 ½ cups mashed potatoes*
2 cups cheese, shredded
¾ cup onion, chopped
4 cloves garlic, chopped
½ cup carrot, chopped
1 tablespoon coconut oil, butter, or lard
⅓ cup green beans
½ pound ground beef
1 tablespoon cornstarch or arrowroot flour
¾ cup water
¼ teaspoon salt
⅛ teaspoon pepper
¼ teaspoon paprika
4 unbaked single-crust tart pastry shells (page 117)

Prepare mashed potatoes. Stir cheese into potatoes and set aside. Sauté onion, garlic, and carrot in oil until tender crisp. Add green beans and ground beef and cook until meat is lightly browned. Mix cornstarch in water and stir into meat mixture, stirring constantly until thickened. Add salt, pepper, and paprika; reduce heat and simmer for about 5 minutes. Fill tart shells with hot mixture. Spoon mashed potatoes on top. Bake at 400 degrees F (205 C) for 18 minutes. Serve with a pat of butter on top of each pie.

* Mashed cauliflower may be substituted for the mashed potatoes. Cook 1½ cups of chopped cauliflower until very tender. Add 1 tablespoon butter, ⅛ teaspoon salt, and mash. Stir in cheese and follow instructions as directed above.

CHICKEN POT PIE

This is an easy recipe because it uses only the top crust of the pastry shell. If you prefer, you can make it using a double-crust.

2 cups cut-up chicken
3 cups chicken broth
1 stalk celery, chopped
1 medium carrot, chopped
1 cup onion, chopped
2 medium potatoes, chopped*
½ cup peas
½ teaspoon salt
⅛ teaspoon pepper
¼ teaspoon basil
⅛ teaspoon thyme
2 teaspoons cornstarch or arrowroot flour
½ cup coconut milk
6 uncooked tart pastry shell tops (page 117)

In a large saucepan bring chicken broth to a boil. Add chicken, celery, carrot, and onion; reduce heat, cover, and simmer for 30 minutes. Add potatoes and peas and simmer for an additional 30 minutes or until vegetables are tender. Add salt, pepper, basil, and thyme. Mix together cornstarch and coconut milk and stir into stew. Continue to cook for 5 minutes or until thickened. Pour hot stew into tart pastry pans. Add top crust. Make a couple of slits in crust to allow steam to escape. Bake on cookie sheet at 400 degrees F (205 C) for 15 minutes.

*One cup of chopped cauliflower can be substituted for the potatoes.

BEEF POT PIE

This recipe is easy to make because it uses only the top crust of the pastry shell. You can also make it using a double-crust if desired.

1 pound stew beef, cup into bite-size pieces
¾ cup onion, chopped

1 medium carrot, chopped
½ cup green beans
¼ cup tomato sauce
1 tablespoon coconut oil, butter, or lard
2 tablespoons cornstarch or arrowroot flour
½ teaspoon salt
⅛ teaspoon pepper
⅛ teaspoon paprika
⅛ teaspoon thyme
6 unbaked tart pastry shell tops (page 117)

In large saucepan bring 2 cups water to a boil. Add beef, onion, carrot, green beans, and tomato sauce. Reduce heat, cover, and simmer for 60 minutes. Mix cornstarch in ¼ cup water and stir into meat mixture, stirring constantly until thickened. Add salt and spices and simmer for about 5 minutes. Fill tart pans with hot mixture. Add top crust. Cut slits in crust or puncture with a fork to allow steam to escape. Bake on cookie sheet at 400 degrees F (205 C) for 15 minutes.

CHICKEN BROCCOLI POT PIE

3 tablespoons butter
1 cup cut-up chicken
½ cup onion, chopped
4 cups broccoli, chopped
½ cup coconut milk
1½ cups cheese, shredded
½ teaspoon salt
⅛ teaspoon pepper
4 unbaked double-crust tart pastry shells (page 148)

In large saucepan sauté butter, chicken, onion, and broccoli until vegetables are tender. Reduce heat, add coconut milk, cheese, salt, and pepper and cook until cheese is melted. Fill tart shells with hot mixture. Add top crust. Cut slits in top crust or puncture with a fork to allow steam to escape. Bake on cookie sheet at 400 degrees F (205 C) for 15 minutes.

STUFFED MUSHROOMS

10-12 medium mushrooms
1½ teaspoon onion, finely chopped
1½ teaspoon butter
2 tablespoons coconut flour
2 tablespoons coconut milk
1 tablespoon fresh parsley, finely chopped
Dash nutmeg
⅛ teaspoon salt
⅛ teaspoon pepper
Parmesan cheese, grated

Clean and dry mushrooms. Remove and finely chop the stems. Set mushroom caps aside. Sauté mushroom stems and onion in butter until tender. Remove from heat and mix in coconut flour, coconut milk, parsley, nutmeg, salt, and pepper. Fill cavity of each mushroom cap and top with grated Parmesan cheese. Bake at 425 degrees F (225 C) for 15 minutes.

ROASTED GARLIC BEAN DIP

2 heads garlic, roasted
2 cans (15 ounces each) white beans, drained
¼ cup extra virgin olive oil
4 teaspoons ground cumin
½ cup lemon juice
¼ cup coconut milk
2 teaspoons fresh rosemary
2 teaspoons fresh oregano
2 teaspoons fresh thyme
3 tablespoons coconut flour

Puree all ingredients in food processor. Add more liquid if necessary to achieve desired consistency. Serve with chips, cracker, fresh carrot or celery sticks.

HUMMUS

Hummus makes an appetizing high fiber spread or dip.

1 can (25 ounces) or 2½ cups cooked garbanzo beans, reserve liquid
¼ cup olive oil
¼ cup tahini
¼ cup lemon juice
3 cloves garlic
1 teaspoon salt
¼ cup fresh parsley, chopped
½ teaspoon crushed red pepper
¼ teaspoon ground cumin
¼ cup sifted coconut flour

Blend all ingredients in food processor. Add reserved liquid drained from beans as needed to achieve desired consistency.

Appendix

Resources

Dr. Fife's Non-Stick Cooking Oil, Coconut Flour, and Other Coconut Products

Fresh and dried coconut and coconut milk are available at most grocery stores. Coconut milk is usually sold in the Asian or Ethnic Foods section. Most all coconut products including coconut oil, coconut fiber, and coconut flour are available in health food stores. Dr. Fife's Non-Stick Cooking Oil is also available in many health food stores. If you local store does not carry these products ask them to do so. If you cannot find these products in your area, you can get them by mail. For information on how to obtain these products by mail call my free Coconut Directory Service at 719-550-9887.

Coconut Research Center

The Coconut Research Center is a nonprofit organization dedicated to educating the medical community and general public about the health aspects of coconut. The website www.coconutresearchcenter.org contains numerous articles, current research, nutritional information, resources for educational materials and products, and includes an open discussion forum. By far the best and most accurate coconut information resource available on the Internet.

Celiac Disease Support Groups

For the most recent and accurate information about celiac disease or to find local support groups, contact the following organizations:

American Celiac Society, P.O. Box 23455, New Orleans, LA 70183-0455, USA; phone (504) 737-3293; americanceliacsociety@yahoo.com.

Canadian Celiac Association, phone (905) 507-6208, (800) 363-7296; www.celiac.ca.

Celiac.com, P.O. Box 279, Gradena, CA 90248, USA; phone (707) 537-3011; www.celiac.com.

Celiac Disease Foundation, 13251 Ventura Blvd., Suite 1, Studio City, CA 91604-1838, USA; phone (818) 990-2354; www.celiac.org.

Celiac Sprue Association/United States of America (CSA/USA), P.O. Box 31700, Omaha, NE 68131-070, USA; phone (402) 558-0600; www.csaceliacs.org.

Celiacs, Inc., P.O. Box 31144, Omaha, NE 68131, USA; phone (402) 553-3265; www.e-celiacs.org.

Gluten Intolerance Group of North America (GIG), P.O. Box 23053, Broadway Station, Seattle, WA 98102-0353, USA; phone (206) 325-6980; www.gluten.net.

The Coeliac Society of Australia; www.coeliac.org.au.

Coeliac UK, P.O. Box 220, High Wycombe, Bucks, HP11 2HY, UK; phone 0870-444-8804; www.coeliac.co.uk.

Internet's Celiac Conference. Send e-mail to: celiac@ispace.com.

University of Maryland Center for Celiac Research, 20 Penn Street, Room S303B, Baltimore, MD 21201, USA; phone (410) 706-8021; www.celiaccenter.org.

Bibliography

The following books are available from Piccadilly Books, Ltd., P.O. Box 25203, Colorado Springs, CO 80936, USA. Call (719) 550-9887 or e-mail orders@piccadillybooks.com for information or go to www.piccadillybooks.com.

Coconut Cures: Preventing and Treating Common Health Problems with Coconut. Bruce Fife, 2005: Piccadilly Books, Colorado Springs, CO.

Eat Fat, Look Thin: A Safe and Natural way to Lose Weight Permanently, 2nd Ed. Bruce Fife, 2005: Piccadilly Books, Colorado Springs, CO.

The Coconut Oil Miracle, 4th Ed. Bruce Fife, 2004: Avery, New York.

Coconut Lover's Cookbook. Bruce Fife, 2004: Piccadilly Books, Colorado Springs, CO.

Index

CPSIA information can be obtained at www.ICGtesting.com
Printed in the USA
LVOW120827260212

270413LV00006B/77/P